Fodor's POCKET 2001

phoenix &
scottsdale

Excerpted from *Fodor's Arizona 2001*

fodor's travel publications
new york · toronto · london · sydney · auckland

www.fodors.com

contents

maps

ON THE ROAD WITH FODOR'S

EVERY VACATION IS IMPORTANT. So here at Fodor's, we've pulled out all stops in preparing *Fodor's Pocket Phoenix & Scottsdale*. To guide you in putting together your Phoenix & Scottsdale experience, we've created multiday itineraries and regional tours. And to direct you to the places that are truly worth your time and money, we've rallied the team of endearingly picky know-it-alls we're pleased to call our writers. Having seen all corners of Phoenix and Scottsdale, they're real experts. If you knew them, you'd poll them for tips yourself.

No fan of moderate climates, Phoenix updater **Cara LaBrie** left her native Phoenix for Minnesota to cover sports for the St. *Paul Pioneer Press*. She returns regularly to have dinner at her favorite Mexican restaurant and pick oranges from trees in her old backyard.

Editor **David Downing** visited America's greatest natural wonder, the Grand Canyon, for the first time on a family trip in 1968. Today he lives and works in America's greatest unnatural wonder, New York City, where the park rangers just aren't as nice.

Don't Forget to Write

Keeping a travel guide fresh and up-to-date is a big job. So we love your feedback—positive and negative—and follow up on all suggestions. Contact the Phoenix and Scottsdale editor at editors@fodors.com or c/o Fodor's, 280 Park Avenue, New York, New York 10017. And have a wonderful trip!

Karen Cure

Karen Cure

Editorial Director

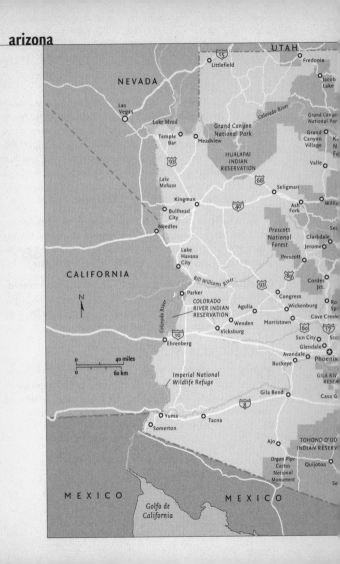

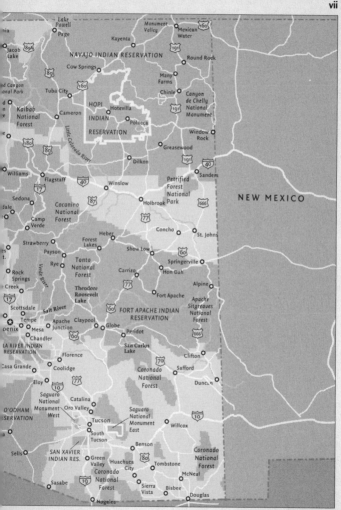

phoenix &
scottsdale

In This Chapter

introducing phoenix and scottsdale

THE EVER-WIDENING PHOENIX metropolitan area is a melding of 22 communities and, with a population of more than a million people, the sixth-largest city in the United States. America's fastest-growing urban center provides a tremendous variety of activities—from golfing on championship courses and hiking on some of the country's most popular trails to dining on the ultimate in Southwest cuisine and luxuriating at world-class resorts. Scottsdale and the college town of Tempe are packed with great boutiques and art galleries. Outside of metropolitan Phoenix, Wickenburg is an authentic Old West town, and the Apache Trail drive is one of the most scenic routes in America.

Phoenix and Scottsdale lie in the heart of central Arizona in the Valley of the Sun—named for its 330-plus days of sunshine each year and giving metro Phoenix its nickname, the Valley. This 1,000-square-mi valley is the northern tip of the Sonoran Desert, a rolling expanse of prehistoric seabed that stretches from central Arizona deep into northwestern Mexico. The landscape of the valley can be surprising for those who don't realize just how lush the desert can be. It's studded with cacti, palo verde trees, and creosote bushes, crusted with hard-baked clay and rock, and scorched by summer temperatures that can stay above 100°F for weeks at a time. But its dry skin responds magically to the touch of rainwater. Spring is a miracle of stately saguaro cacti crowned with white flowers, gold and orange poppies, scarlet blossoms bursting from the dry spikes of the ocotillo, hills ablaze with bright yellow creosote, reddish lavender dotting the antlers of the staghorn cholla, and tiny blue flowers clustering on the stems of the desert sage.

The modern-day populating of this desert benefited from centuries of forethought. As the Hohokam people discovered 2,300 years ago, the springtime rains can be augmented by human hands. Having migrated north from northwestern Mexico, they cultivated cotton, corn, and beans in tilled, rowed, and irrigated fields for about 1,700 years, establishing more than 300 mi of canals—an engineering miracle, particularly when you consider the limited technology available. The Hohokam, whose name comes from the Piman word for "people who have gone before," constructed a great town upon whose ruins modern Phoenix is built—and then vanished.

From the time the Hohokam left until the American Civil War, the once fertile Salt River valley lay forgotten, used only by occasional small bands of Pima and Maricopa peoples. Then, in 1865, the U.S. Army established Fort McDowell in the mountains to the east, where the Verde River flows into the Salt. To feed the men and the horses stationed there, Jack Swilling, a former Confederate army officer, had the idea of reopening the Hohokam canals in 1867. Within a year, fields bright with barley and pumpkins earned the area the name of Punkinsville. But by 1870, when the town was plotted, the 300 inhabitants had decided that their new city would rise "like a phoenix" from the ashes of a vanished civilization.

Phoenix indeed grew steadily. Within 20 years, it had become large enough—at about 3,000 people—to wrest the title of territorial capital from Prescott. By 1912, when Arizona was admitted as a state, the area, irrigated by the brand-new Roosevelt Dam and Salt River Project, had a burgeoning cotton industry. Copper and cattle were mined and raised elsewhere but were banked and traded in Phoenix, and the cattle were slaughtered and packed here in the largest stockyards outside Chicago.

Meanwhile, the climate, so long a crippling liability, became an asset. Desert air was the prescribed therapy for the respiratory ills rampant in the sooty, factory-filled East' Scottsdale began in 1901 as "30-odd tents and a half dozen adobe houses" put up by health seekers. By 1930, visitors looking for warm winter recreation as well as rejuvenating aridity filled the elegant San Marcos Hotel and Arizona Biltmore, first of many of the luxury retreats for which the area is now known worldwide.

Phoenix's main growth spurt occurred in the early 1950s when air-conditioning made summers bearable, and the city has experienced the ups and downs of unbridled growth ever since. It's very much a work still in progress; so much is changing, and so quickly, that even long-time residents have a difficult time keeping up. But at the same time, Phoenix and Scottsdale are low-key places where people take things easy and dress informally. If the heat can be a little overwhelming at the height of a summer day, at least it has the salutary effect of slowing the pace of life down to an enjoyable speed. As old desert hands say, you don't begin to see the desert until you've looked at it long enough to see its colors; and you aren't ready to get up and move until you've seen the sun go down.

PLEASURES AND PASTIMES

Dining

Generations of Phoenix schoolchildren have learned about Arizona's four C's: copper, cattle, cotton, and climate. Today, a good argument could be made for adding a fifth C: cuisine. For years, eating out in Phoenix meant an encounter either with the tacos and burritos of northern Mexico or with the steak and potatoes favored by the city's midwestern transplants. For the truly adventurous, the city had a smattering of Chinese restaurants. Gourmet dining? Funky ethnic eateries? You had a better chance of seeing snow in July.

During the 1980s and 1990s, however, Phoenix's explosive growth fueled a dramatic culinary boom. Creative chefs working with local ingredients took part in the birth of something called southwestern cooking. They started combining familiar, and sometimes not so familiar, flavors in surprising new ways (polenta topped with wild mushrooms in ancho chili cream sauce), reinventing traditional preparations (quesadillas filled with duck and smoked Gouda), and introducing new ingredients (curried-lamb-stuffed tamales with peanut sauce).

Phoenix's expansion also saw the arrival of immigrants from around the world, who brought their cuisines to the Valley of the Sun. Southeast Asian immigrants introduced spicy Asian dishes that were instantly welcome in a city accustomed to fiery chiles. Immigrants from Central America and the Middle East brought more variations on familiar themes. Phoenicians can now enjoy everything from tandoori to sushi. At the same time, an increasingly sophisticated dining public fills tables at high-end American, Continental, French, and Italian spots around town. Still, Phoenix has not forgotten its culinary roots. Steak and Mexican food have never gone out of style, and here in the Southwest, they never will.

Golf

Phoenix is a golf mecca, thanks to the warm weather, azure skies, and serene vistas of the desert. The explosive growth of the area has brought lots of new courses to the Valley over the past two decades, many world-class. The city provides an impressive array of courses—golfers may choose lush, manicured fairways with tranquil lakes and fountains or get right out in the wild dunes and scrub brush of the desert.

Hot-Air Ballooning

For a bird's-eye view of the spectacular desert landscape, try a hot-air balloon ride. The peaceful silence hundreds of feet up is unforgettable; since the balloon is carried on the wind, you'll experience no wind yourself. And an added bonus is that you'll see many elusive desert creatures that can be viewed in their natural habitats only from a balloon.

Lodging

If there's one thing the Valley of the Sun knows how to do right, it's lodging. Metropolitan Phoenix has accommodations ranging from world-class resorts to roadside motels, from upscale dude ranches to no-frills family-style operations where you can do your own cooking.

In This Chapter

Updated by Cara LaBrie

here and there

THE SUN BELT BOOM BEGAN when low-cost air-conditioning made summer heat bearable. From 1950 to 1990, the Phoenix urban area more than quadrupled in population, catapulting real estate and home building into two of the state's biggest industries. Cities planted around Phoenix have become its suburbs, and land that for decades produced cotton and citrus now produces microchips and homes. Glendale and Peoria on the west side, and Tempe, Mesa, Chandler, and Gilbert on the east, make up the nation's third-largest silicon valley.

Numbers in the text correspond to numbers in the margin and on the Downtown and the Cultural Center and Exploring Scottsdale maps.

PHOENIX

DOWNTOWN PHOENIX

The renovated downtown area gives you a look at Phoenix's past and present, as well as a peek at its future. Restored homes from the original townsite give you an idea of how far the city has come since its inception around the turn of the last century, and several fine museums point to the Valley of the Sun's increasing sophistication in the coming one.

A Good Walk

Park your car in the garage on the southeast corner of 5th and Monroe streets or at any of the many nearby public parking

facilities (they're listed on the free map provided by Downtown Phoenix Partnership and available in local restaurants). Begin your tour in the blocks known as the Heritage and Science Park; 5th to 7th streets between Monroe and Adams contain **Heritage Square** ①, the **Arizona Science Center** ②, and the **Phoenix Museum of History** ③. From the corner of 5th and Monroe, walk two blocks west to **St. Mary's Basilica** ④, Phoenix's first

Catholic church. Head north one block to Van Buren Street. On the northeast corner of the intersection, you'll see two glass-clad office towers with a lane of royal palms between them. Follow the palm trees: they lead to the **Arizona Center** ⑤. Leaving the Arizona Center, from the corner of 3rd and Van Buren, walk a block west to 2nd Street and two blocks south on 2nd Street, passing the 24-story Hyatt Regency hotel on your right, then another block and a half west on Adams Street to the **Museo Chicano** ⑥. You can walk to Heritage and Science Park from here, catch a DASH shuttle back, or continue on two more blocks west toward the striking facade of the **Orpheum Theatre** ⑦.

If you're really an indefatigable walker, continue south through the plaza on the Orpheum's east side to Washington Street; head east on Washington Street, passing Historic City Hall and the county courthouse on your right. At the intersection of Washington Street and 1st Avenue, you'll see Patriots Square Park on the southeast corner; cross diagonally (southeast) through the park to the corner of Jefferson Street and Central Avenue. Another block east on Jefferson and then a block south on 1st Street will take you to the site of the **America West Arena** ⑧. From the arena, follow Jefferson Street east for two blocks to South 4th Avenue and Phoenix's newest sports venue, **Bank One Ballpark** ⑨. Afterward, catch the DASH shuttle back to your car.

TIMING

In moderate weather, this walk is a pleasant daylong tour; from late May to mid-October, it's best to break it up over two days. Be sure to take advantage of the 35¢ DASH (Downtown Area Shuttle; ☞ Bus Travel in Practical Information).

Sights to See

❽ **AMERICA WEST ARENA.** This 20,000-seat sports palace is the home of the Phoenix Suns NBA team, the Arizona Rattlers arena

downtown and the cultural center

football team, the Phoenix Mercury professional women's basketball team, and the Phoenix Coyotes NHL team. Almost a mall in itself—with cafés and shops, in addition to the team offices—it's interesting to tour even when there's no game on. Check out the video art in the lobby, including the three robot figures fashioned out of small televisions. Tours cost $3, but availability is determined by the arena's schedule of events. Call for current times. *201 E. Jefferson St., at 2nd St., tel. 602/379–2000.*

❺ **ARIZONA CENTER.** Beyond an oasis of dramatic fountains and sunken gardens stands the curved, two-tiered structure that is downtown's most astonishing shopping venue. The first thing you'll see is the Hooter's at the entrance, which in a way sets the tone for the entire mall. More energetically cheesy than truly elegant, the center boasts a variety of souvenir shops (some with nice merchandise), a dozen restaurants spread over two stories, the state's largest sports bar, and delightful palms, pools, and fountains. There is a variety of chain and specialty stores as well as open-air vendors stationed in the plaza. *Van Buren St. between 3rd and 5th Sts., tel. 602/271–4000 or 480/949–4386.*

★ ❷ **ARIZONA SCIENCE CENTER.** This concrete monolith, designed by Antoine Predock, is *the* Phoenix venue for science-related fun and exploration. Lively "please touch" exhibits provide an entertaining educational experience for kids and grown-ups alike—learn about the physics of making gigantic soap bubbles, the technology of satellite weather systems, the launching of hot-air balloons, or how to spin like a figure skater, and listen in to the control tower at Sky Harbor airport. Under the dome of Dorrance Planetarium, dazzling computer graphics simulate orbits and eclipses, as well as three-dimensional space flight. The Irene P. Flinn theater has a 50-ft-high projection screen where such films as "Wolves" and "To Be an Astronaut" are presented in I-WORKS, an IMAX-type technology. *600 E. Washington St., tel. 602/*

716–2000. Museum $8; combination museum, theater, and planetarium $11. Daily 10–5.

❾ BANK ONE BALLPARK. Known affectionately as BOB, the Valley's new major league ballpark is home to the Arizona Diamondbacks. Complete with a retractable roof and even a right field swimming pool, BOB lets Phoenicians enjoy a day at the ballpark while escaping the summer heat. Tours of the state-of-the-art facility are given on non-game days, Monday through Saturday, at 10:30, noon, 1:30, and 3. On game days, tours are scheduled at 10:30 and noon only. At all times, it's a good idea to reserve in advance. 401 E. Jefferson St., between S. 4th and S. 7th Sts., tel. 602/462–6000. Tours $6.

❶ HERITAGE SQUARE. In a parklike setting from 5th to 7th streets between Monroe and Adams, this city-owned block contains the only remaining homes from the original Phoenix townsite. On the south side of the square, along Adams Street, stand several houses built between 1899 and 1901. The Midwestern-style **Stevens House** holds the **Arizona Doll and Toy Museum** (602 E. Adams St., tel. 602/253–9337). The **Teeter House,** the third house in the row, is a Victorian-style tearoom. The **Silva House** (tel. 602/236–5451), a bungalow from 1900, has presentations about turn-of-the-century life for settlers in the Phoenix township. On the south side of Adams Street in the **Thomas House** and **Baird Machine Shop** is an Italian bakery/pizzeria combination, **Bianco's** (☞ Eating Out).

The queen of Heritage Square is the **Rosson House,** an 1895 Victorian in the Queen Anne style. Built by a physician who served a brief term as mayor, it is the sole survivor of the fewer than two dozen Victorians erected in Phoenix. It was bought and restored by the city in 1974. A 30-minute tour of this classic is worth the modest admission price. 6th and Monroe Sts., tel. 602/495–7000. $3. Wed.–Sat. 10–3:30, Sun. noon–3:30.

NEED A BREAK? The Victorian-style tearoom in the **Teeter House** (622 E. Adams St., tel. 602/252–4682) serves such authentic tea-time fare as Devonshire cream, scones with berries, and cucumber sandwiches. Heartier gourmet sandwiches and salads are also available. The staff will happily box any of your choices, should you prefer to enjoy them on the lawn outside.

6 MUSEO CHICANO. Artistic works of artists from both the United States and Mexico are showcased here. Exhibits display the broad range of classic and modern culture, making this site one of the premier centers for contemporary Latin American art. 147 E. Adams St., tel. 602/257–5536. $2. Tues.–Sat. 10–4.

7 ORPHEUM THEATRE. The Spanish-colonial–revival architecture and exterior reliefs of this 1929 movie palace have long been admired, and now, after an extensive renovation by artisans and craftspeople, the eclectic ornamental details of the interior have been meticulously restored. Call for details on guided tours and upcoming events. 203 W. Adams St., tel. 602/495–7000.

★ ☙ **3 PHOENIX MUSEUM OF HISTORY.** This striking glass-and-steel museum offers a healthy dose of regional history from the 1860s (when Anglo settlement began) through the 1930s. A tour through interactive exhibits allows guests to appreciate the city's multicultural heritage as well as witness its growth. You're invited to play Sniff That Barrel (to guess its contents) at a replica of Hancock Store (an 1860s Circle-K equivalent) or take a turn at packing a toy wagon with color-coded blocks as if for a cross-country trip. 105 N. 5th St., tel. 602/253–2734. $5. Mon.–Sat. 10–5, Sun. noon–5.

4 ST. MARY'S BASILICA. Founded in 1881, Phoenix's first Catholic church presents a stunning facade, its pink stucco and twin towers a pleasant anomaly among the modern concrete of downtown. Inside, the basilica, where Pope John Paul II visited in 1987, has magnificent stained-glass windows designed in Munich. Mass is held daily, but call the parish office for visiting hours. *N. 3rd and Monroe Sts., tel. 602/252–7651. Free. Hrs vary, call for opening times.*

THE CULTURAL CENTER

The heart of Phoenix's downtown cultural center is the rolling greensward of the Margaret T. Hance Park, also known as Deck Park. Built atop the I–10 tunnel under Central Avenue, it spreads more than 1 mi from 3rd Avenue on the west to 3rd Street on the east, and ¼ mi from Portland Street north to Culver Street. It is the city's second-largest downtown park (the largest is half-century-old Encanto Park, 2 mi northwest). Deck Park is a good place from which to survey revitalized downtown neighborhoods and to appreciate the expansions and renovations of nearly all the area's museums.

A Good Walk

Park free in the lot of the **Phoenix Central Library** ⑩ at the corner of Central Avenue and East Willetta Street. Two blocks north on Central, across McDowell Road, is the modern, green-quartz structure of the **Phoenix Art Museum** ⑪. North of the museum, a slight detour brings a brief respite from the noise and traffic of Central Avenue as well as a glimpse of some lovely residential architecture: head one block east on Coronado Road to Alvarado Road, then follow Alvarado north for two longish blocks (zigzagging a few feet to the east at Palm Lane) to Monte Vista Road; turn left onto Monte Vista and proceed 50 yards west to the entrance of the **Heard Museum** ⑫. From the Heard, head south on Central Avenue toward the red-granite Viad Tower, with its refreshing fountains and intriguing sculpture garden.

TIMING

Seeing all of the neighborhood's attractions makes a comfortable day tour in moderate weather; in the warm months, it is too much for one day. Bus o runs up and down Central Avenue every 10 minutes on weekdays and every 20 minutes on Saturday.

Sights to See

★ ✋ ⑫ **HEARD MUSEUM.** Pioneer Phoenix settlers Dwight and Maie Heard had a Spanish-colonial–revival building erected on their property to house their impressive collection of Southwestern art; today, the site has developed into the nation's premier showcase of Native American art, basketry, pottery, weavings, and bead work. Children will enjoy the interactive art-making exhibits, and events such as the Guild Indian Fair and the Hoop Dancing Competition explore the Native American experience. The museum also has the best gift shop in town; it's not cheap, but you can be sure you're getting authentic, high-quality goods. 2301 N. Central Ave., tel. 602/252–8848 or 602/252–8840. $6. Mon.–Sat. 9:30–5, Sun. noon–5.

. . . .

NEED A BREAK? The grassy park of the **Viad Corporate Center,** on Central Avenue between McDowell Road and Palm Lane, is a great place to stop for a rest. A string of tiered fountains snakes through the 2-acre park and sculpture garden, which contains a collection of lifelike works in bronze—some so realistic, you might unwittingly pass right by them. Stop to appreciate their whimsical touches, such as the blue-capped window washer's paperback copy of *Rear Window* tucked in his overalls.

. . . .

⑪ **PHOENIX ART MUSEUM.** The green-quartz exterior of this modern museum is another eye-catching piece of architecture on Central Avenue. More than 13,000 objets d'art are on display inside, including 18th- and 19th-century European works and the American West collection, which features painters from Frederic Remington to Georgia O'Keeffe. A clothing-and-costume collection has pieces from 1750, and the Asian art gallery is filled with fine Chinese porcelain and pieces of intricate cloisonné. 1625 N. Central Ave., tel. 602/257–1880. $6; tours free. Mon.–Wed. and weekends 10–5, Thurs.–Fri. 10–9.

⑩ PHOENIX CENTRAL LIBRARY. Architect Will Bruder's magnificent 1995 contribution to Central Avenue is absolutely worth a stop. The curved building's copper-penny exterior evokes images of the region's sunburnt mesas; inside, skylights, glass walls, and mirrors keep the structure bathed in natural light. A five-story glass atrium, known as the Crystal Canyon, is best appreciated from a speedy ride in one of three glass elevators. At the top, from the largest reading room in North America, check out a cable-suspended steel ceiling that appears to float overhead. Free one-hour tours are offered on Friday; call to arrange one in advance. *1221 N. Central Ave., tel. 602/262–4636; 602/262–6582 tour reservations. Mon.–Thurs. 9–9, Fri.–Sat. 9–6, Sun. 1–5.*

NEED A BREAK? Funky, friendly **Willow House** (149 W. McDowell Rd., tel. 602/252–0272) is the area's most comfortable coffeehouse. Grab a sandwich, dessert, or coffee and stretch out in a low-slung couch underneath brightly painted walls. Check out the various art works on display, as well as the kaleidoscopic fish swimming along the rest room walls.

SOUTH PHOENIX

A mostly residential area and home to much of Phoenix's substantial Hispanic population, South Phoenix is worth a visit for two reasons: its family-style restaurants and roadside stands offer some of the best Mexican food in the city, and it's home to South Mountain Park and the Mystery Castle, two of Phoenix's most remarkable sights.

A Good Drive

From central Phoenix, take 7th Street south, past Baseline Road, to the junction of Mineral Road and 7th Street. There you'll find the **Mystery Castle,** a decidedly original home-turned-minimuseum. After a tour, follow Mineral Road west for about ½ mi to Central Avenue and the entrance to **South Mountain Park.**

Take any of several scenic drives through this 16,500-acre city-owned wilderness. Labeled as "the most romantic view" in the park is Dobbins Lookout, from which you can survey the surrounding peaks and valleys. Maps of all scenic drives as well as of hiking, mountain biking, and horseback trails are available at the Gatehouse Entrance just inside the park boundary.

TIMING

Depending on how long you spend in the park, this tour can be accomplished in a couple of hours or can last an entire day. Leave about a half hour each way for driving, an hour to 90 minutes at the castle, and anywhere from a quick 20-minute drive to an all-day hike in South Mountain.

Sights to See

★ **MYSTERY CASTLE.** At the foot of South Mountain lies a curious dwelling fashioned from desert rocks, railroad refuse, and anything else its builder, Boyce Gulley, could get his hands on. Boyce's daughter Mary Lou lives here now and leads tours on request. Full of fascinating oddities, the castle has 18 rooms with 13 fireplaces, a downstairs grotto tavern, and a roll-away bed with a mining railcar as its frame. The pump organ belonged to Elsie, the Widow of Tombstone, who buried six husbands under suspicious circumstances. *800 E. Mineral Rd., tel. 602/268–1581. $4. Oct.–June, Thurs.–Sun. 11–4.*

★ **SOUTH MOUNTAIN PARK.** This desert wonderland, the world's largest city park (almost 17,000 acres), offers an outdoor experience unparalleled in the Valley: a wilderness of mountain/desert trails (☞ Hiking *in* Outdoor Activities and Sports) for hikers, bikers, and horseback riders. The Environmental Center features a large relief model of the park as well as displays detailing the park's history, from the time of the ancient Hohokam peoples to that of gold-seeking adventurers. Roads climb past buildings constructed by the Civilian Conservation Corps during the New Deal Era, winding through desert flora to the trailheads; scenic overlooks reveal the distant Phoenix skyline, which seems a world away from this wild and luxuriant oasis. Look for ancient petroglyphs, try to spot a desert cottontail rabbit or chuckwalla lizard, or simply stroll among the wondrous vegetation. It's an electrifying experience, all the more startling for being placed right on the edge of a major metropolis. *10919 S. Central Ave., tel. 602/495–0222. Free. Daily 5:30 AM–10:30 PM. Environmental Center Mon.–Sat. 9–5, Sun. noon–5. Group tours and educational programs available by advance reservation only.*

NEED A BREAK? For a break from Mexican food, check out the Texas-style ribs, brisket, and chicken at **Black's Smokey Hog BBQ** (2010 E. Broadway Rd., tel. 602/305–9693). If you're feeling presidential, stop by **Poncho's** (7202 S. Central Ave., tel. 602/276–2437), where Bill Clinton enjoyed the Fiesta Chiquita, a sampler platter of chimichangas, tacos, tamales, tostadas, and frijoles. Be sure to load up on fresh sopaipillas (a warm pocket of pancake-like bread) brought to you by your server when you raise the Mexican flag at your table. They're especially good with honey poured inside.

PAPAGO SALADO

The word "Papago," meaning "bean eater," was a name given by 16th-century Spanish explorers to the Hohokam (as they are more properly called), a vanished native people of the Phoenix area. Farmers of the desert, the Hohokam grew corn, beans, squash, and cotton. They lived in central Arizona from about AD 1 to 1450, at which point their civilization collapsed and disappeared for reasons unknown, abandoning the Salt River (Rio Salado) Valley and leaving behind remains of villages and a complex system of irrigation canals. The Papago Salado region is between Phoenix and Tempe and contains the Pueblo Grande ruins, the Desert Botanical Garden, the Phoenix Zoo, and various recreational opportunities amid the buttes of Papago Park.

A Good Drive

From downtown Phoenix, take Washington Street east to the **Pueblo Grande Museum and Cultural Park,** between 44th Street and the Hohokam Expressway (AZ 143). After a stop at the museum, follow Washington Street east 3½ mi to Priest Drive and turn north. Priest Drive becomes Galvin Parkway north of Van Buren Street; follow signs to entrances for the **Phoenix Zoo** and **Papago Park,** or to the **Desert Botanical Garden.** To visit the **Hall of Flame** afterward, drive south on Galvin Parkway to Van Buren Street; turn east on Van Buren and drive ⅛ mi, turning south onto Project Drive (at the buff-color stone marker that reads SALT RIVER PROJECT).

TIMING

Seeing all the sights requires the better part of a day. You may want to save the Desert Botanical Garden for the end of your tour, as it stays open 8–8 year-round and is particularly lovely when lighted by the setting sun or by moonlight.

Sights to See

★ ✋ **DESERT BOTANICAL GARDEN.** Opened in 1939 to conserve and showcase the ecology of the desert, these 150 acres contain more than 4,000 different species of cacti, succulents, trees, and flowers. A stroll along the ½-mi-long "Plants and People of the Sonoran Desert" trail is a fascinating lesson in environmental adaptations; children will enjoy playing the self-guiding game "Desert Detective." *1201 N. Galvin Pkwy., tel. 602/941–1217 or 480/941–1225. $7.50. Oct.–Apr., daily 8–8; May–Sept., daily 7 AM–8 PM.*

NEED A BREAK? If you're headed to the Papago Salado region from downtown Phoenix, stop in **Kohnie's Coffee** (4225 E. Camelback Rd., tel.

602/952–9948) for coffee, pastries, bagels, and scones. It's open at 7 AM (8 AM Sunday) and closed by 1 PM (noon on weekends).

🔆 **HALL OF FLAME.** Retired firefighters lead tours through more than 100 restored fire engines and tell harrowing tales of the "world's most dangerous profession." Kids can climb on a 1916 engine, operate alarm systems, and learn lessons of fire safety from the pros. More than 3,000 helmets, badges, and other firefighting-related articles are on display, dating from as far back as 1725. 6101 E. Van Buren St., tel. 602/275–3473. $5. Mon.–Sat. 9–5, Sun. noon–4.

Papago Park. An amalgam of hilly desert terrain, streams, and lagoons, this park has picnic ramadas (shaded, open air shelters), a playground, hiking and biking trails, and even largemouth bass and trout fishing. (An urban fishing license is required for anglers age 15 and over; you can pick one up at sporting-goods or Circle-K stores.) The hike up to landmark **Hole-in-the-Rock** is popular—but remember that it's much easier to climb up to the hole than to get down. **Governor Hunt's Tomb,** the white pyramid at the top of Ramada 16, commemorates the former Arizona leader and provides a lovely view. 625 N. Galvin Pkwy., tel. 602/256–3220. Free. Daily 6 AM–10 PM.

OFF THE **BEAD MUSEUM** – When business in the former Prescott location
BEATEN dropped off in 1999, this little museum packed up its wares and
PATH headed for the heart of Glendale, only minutes from downtown Phoenix. Visitors here learn the intriguing story of international trade and intricate bead craft from 30,000 BC through today. There's a gift shop, too. 5754 W. Glenn Dr., tel. 623/930–7395. $3. Mon.–Sat. 10–5, Sun. 11–4.

🔆 **PHOENIX ZOO.** Four designated trails wind through this 125-acre zoo, which has replicas of such habitats as an African savanna and a tropical rain forest. Meerkats, warthogs, desert bighorn sheep, and the endangered Arabian oryx are among the unusual sights, as is Uco, the endangered spectacled bear from South America. The Discovery Trail at Harmony Farm introduces young visitors to small mammals, and a stop at the big red barn provides a chance to help groom goats and sheep. The 30-minute narrated safari train tour costs $2 and provides a good overview of the park. In December, the popular "Zoo Lights" exhibit transforms the area into an enchanted forest of more than 600,000 twinkling lights, many in the shape of the zoo's residents. *455 N. Galvin Pkwy., tel. 602/273–1341. $8.50. Sept.–Apr., daily 9–5; May–Aug., daily 7:30–4.*

★ **PUEBLO GRANDE MUSEUM AND CULTURAL PARK.** Phoenix's only national landmark, this park was once the site of a 500-acre Hohokam village supporting about 1,000 people and containing homes, storage rooms, cemeteries, and several ball courts. Three exhibition galleries hold displays on the Hohokam culture, archaeological methods, and other Southwest themes; kids will like the hands-on, interactive learning center. View the 10-minute orientation video before heading out on the ½-mi Ruin Trail past excavated mounds and ruined structures that give a hint of Hohokam savvy: There's a building whose corner doorway was perfectly placed to watch the summer solstice sunrise. *4619 E. Washington St., tel. 602/495–0901. $2; free Sun. Mon.–Sat. 9–4:45, Sun. 1–4:45.*

SCOTTSDALE

Historic sites, nationally known art galleries, and souvenir shops fill downtown Scottsdale; a quick walking tour can easily turn into an all-day excursion if you browse. Historic Old Town Scottsdale features the look of the Old West, and 5th Avenue is known for shopping and Native American jewelry and crafts stores. Cross onto Main Street and enter a world frequented by the international art set (Scottsdale has the third-largest artist community in the United States); discover more galleries and interior-design shops along Marshall Way (☞ Shopping).

A Good Walk

Park in the free public lot on the corner of 2nd Street and Wells Fargo Avenue, east of Scottsdale Road. A portion of the garage has a three-hour limit; go to upper levels that don't carry time restrictions (enforcement on lower levels is strict).

Start your walk by exiting the parking structure from its northeast corner, where a short brick-paved sidewalk leads northward to the plaza of Scottsdale Mall. You'll immediately come upon the **Scottsdale Center for the Arts** ⑬. Be sure to check out the newest addition to this arts complex, the **Scottsdale Museum of Contemporary Art** ⑭, right next door to the main center building. Stroll counterclockwise around the mall's lovely grounds, passing Scottsdale's library and municipal buildings, and ending up on the plaza's west side by the **Scottsdale Chamber of Commerce** ⑮ and **Scottsdale Historical Museum** ⑯. Continue west to the intersection of Brown Avenue and Main Street to reach the heart of **Old Town Scottsdale** ⑰, occupying four square blocks from Brown Avenue to Scottsdale Road, between Indian School Road and 2nd Street. From Main Street in Old Town, cross Scottsdale Road to the central drag of the **Main Street Arts District** ⑱. Turn north onto Goldwater Boulevard and gallery-stroll for another two blocks. At Indian School Road, head one block east to the **Marshall Way Arts District** ⑲. Continue two blocks north on Marshall Way to the fountain of prancing Arabian horses that marks **5th Avenue** ⑳. You can catch the trolley back to Scottsdale Mall here, on the south side of the intersection of 5th Avenue and Stetson Drive, or walk the five blocks south on Scottsdale Road and one block east on Main Street.

Not far from downtown Scottsdale are three other worthy attractions: the **Buffalo Museum, Taliesin West** (Frank Lloyd

Wright's winter home), and the lovely **Fleischer Museum.** While in this northern area, see the fascinating metal and ceramic wind chimes at Cosanti Originals studio (☞ Shopping), made by disciples of Paolo Soleri, the father of the futuristic Arcosanti.

TIMING

Plan to spend a full day in Scottsdale, as there's a lot to take in between the countless galleries and shops. Although your tour can easily be completed on foot, a trolley runs through the downtown area and out to several resorts: Ollie the Trolley charges $5 for an all-day pass, although service in downtown Scottsdale is free (tel. 480/970–8130 for information). Also look for horse-drawn **Arizona Carriage Company** (tel. 480/423–1449), whose Cinderella-like carriages provide romantic transportation throughout Old Town Scottsdale ($20 for 15-minute tours, $40 for a half hour, $70 for an hour for carriages that hold up to six). They're also perfect props for snapshots.

The best option, if you're interested in touring the galleries, is to visit on a Thursday and do the Scottsdale Art Walk (☞ Arts and Crafts in Shopping).

Sights to See

⓴ 5TH AVENUE. For more than 40 years, this shopping stretch has been home to boutiques and specialty shops. Whether you seek handmade Native American arts and crafts, casual clothing, or cacti, you'll find it here—plus colorful storefronts, friendly merchants, even an old "cigar store" Indian. After a full day of paintings, turquoise jewelry, and knickknacks, children especially may enjoy casting their eyes upon the six-story monster screen of the **IMAX Theater** (4343 N. Scottsdale Rd., tel. 480/945–4629), at the east end of the avenue. *Civic Center Rd. and Stetson Dr.*

OFF THE **BUFFALO MUSEUM OF AMERICA** – Tucked away in a Scottsdale
BEATEN shopping plaza, this eclectic little museum pays homage to the
PATH American bison, or buffalo, and its important role in American

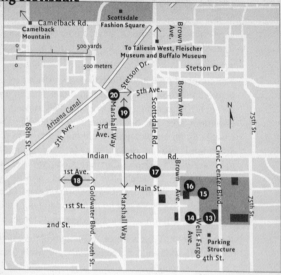

5th Avenue, **20**

Main Street
Arts District, **18**

Marshall Way Arts
District, **19**

Old Town
Scottsdale, **17**

Scottsdale Center
for the Arts, **13**

Scottsdale
Chamber of
Commerce, **15**

Scottsdale
Historical
Museum, **16**

Scottsdale
Museum of
Contemporary
Art, **14**

history. The museum's contents range from the awesome
shaggy beast itself—courtesy of modern taxidermy—to a
variety of original works of fine art, to props from the film *Dances
with Wolves*. The Buffalo Bill Room showcases the legendary
hunter's personal possessions, and the downstairs gift shop is
a mélange of all things buffalo—clocks, banks, tins, plates, old
stereoscope cards, even a promotional poster from Hunter S.

Thompson's novel *Where the Buffalo Roam*. *10261 N. Scottsdale Rd., tel. 480/951–1022. $3. Weekdays 9–5.*

FLEISCHER MUSEUM – Housed in the corporate Perimeter Center, this collection is an undiscovered gem. More than 80 artists from the California School of Impressionism, which is noted for its brightly colored plein-air painting, are represented, including William Wendt and Franz A. Bischoff. It's worth a trip to the somewhat out-of-the-way location. *17207 N. Perimeter Dr., at the intersection of Pima and Bell Rds., tel. 602/585–3108. Free. Daily 10–4. Closed holidays.*

TALIESIN WEST – Ten years after visiting Arizona in 1927 to consult on designs for the Biltmore hotel, architect Frank Lloyd Wright chose 600 acres of raw, rugged Sonoran Desert at the foothills of the McDowell Mountains, just outside Scottsdale, as the site for his permanent winter residence. Wright and apprentices constructed a desert camp here, using what he called organic architecture to integrate the buildings with their natural surroundings. An ingenious harmony of indoor and outdoor space is the result. In addition to the living quarters, drafting studio, and small apartments of the Apprentice Court, Taliesin West also has two theaters, a music pavilion, and the "Sun Trap"—a charming structure of sleeping spaces surrounding an open patio and fireplace. Two guided tours cover different parts of the interior, and a guided "Desert Walk" winds through the petroglyphs and landscape from which Wright drew his vision, as well as the experimental desert residences designed by his apprentices. Tour times vary, so call ahead; all visitors must be accompanied by a guide. *12621 Frank Lloyd Wright Blvd., tel. 480/860–8810 or 480/860–2700. Guided tour (1 hr) $14 winter, $10 summer; Behind the Scenes tour (3 hrs) $35 winter, $25 summer; Desert Walk tour (90 mins) $20. Oct.–May, daily 8:30–5:30; June–Sept., daily 8:30–5.*

★ ⑱ **MAIN STREET ARTS DISTRICT.** Gallery after gallery on Main Street and First Avenue, particularly on the blocks between Scottsdale

Road and 69th Street, displays artwork of myriad styles—contemporary, Western realism, Native American, and traditional. Several antiques shops are also here; specialties include elegant porcelains and china, jewelry, and Oriental rugs.

NEED A BREAK? For a light meal during daytime gallery-hopping, try **Arcadia Farms** (7014 E. 1st Ave., tel. 480/941–5665), where such eclectic fare as raspberry–goat cheese salad and rosemary-seasoned focaccia with chicken, roasted eggplant, and feta cheese are prepared lovingly. Enjoy a cool drink or a justly popular lemon roulade pastry on the brick patio shaded by African sumac trees.

⑲ MARSHALL WAY ARTS DISTRICT. Galleries that exhibit predominantly contemporary art line the blocks of Marshall Way north of Indian School Road. Upscale gift and jewelry stores can be found here, too. Farther north on Marshall Way across 3rd Avenue, the street is filled with more art galleries and creative stores with a Southwestern flair.

⑰ OLD TOWN SCOTTSDALE. Billed as "the West's Most Western Town," this area of Scottsdale has rustic storefronts and wooden sidewalks; it's touristy, but the closest you'll come to experiencing life here as it was 80 years ago. High-quality jewelry, pots, and Mexican imports are sold alongside the expected kitschy souvenirs.

⑬ SCOTTSDALE CENTER FOR THE ARTS. Galleries within this cultural and entertainment complex rotate exhibits frequently, but typically emphasize contemporary art and artists. The airy and bright **Museum Store** (tel. 480/874–4464) has a great collection of unusual jewelry, as well as stationery, posters, and art books. 7380 E. 2nd St., tel. 480/994–2787. Free. Mon.–Sat. 10–5, Thurs. 10–8, Sun. noon–5; also open during performance intermissions.

⑮ **SCOTTSDALE CHAMBER OF COMMERCE.** Pop inside to pick up some local maps, guidebooks, and brochures. Ask the helpful staff for a walking-tour map of Old Town Scottsdale's historic sites. *7343 Scottsdale Mall, tel. 602/945–8481 or 800/877–1117. Weekdays 8:30–6:30, Sat. 10–5, Sun. 11–5.*

⑯ **SCOTTSDALE HISTORICAL MUSEUM.** Scottsdale's first schoolhouse, this redbrick building houses a version of the 1910 schoolroom, as well as photographs, original furniture from the city's founding fathers, and displays of other treasures from Scottsdale's early days. *7333 Scottsdale Mall, tel. 602/945–4499. Free. Wed.–Sat. 10–5, Sun. noon–5. Closed July–Aug.*

⑭ **SCOTTSDALE MUSEUM OF CONTEMPORARY ART.** This museum, next to the Scottsdale Center for the Arts, opened in 1999 in the spectacular Gerard L. Cafesjian Pavilion. When you step through the immense glass entryway designed by New York artist James Fraser Carpenter and stroll through the spaces within the five galleries, you'll realize it's not just the spacious outdoor sculpture garden that makes this a "museum without walls." The opening exhibit featured a variety of contemporary works, including studio glass by Czech artists Stanislav Libensky and Jaroslava Brychtova; mixed-media pieces by Luis Jimenez and William Wegman; and presentations by visual arts performers Jack Massing and Michael Galbreath. New installations are planned every few months, with an emphasis on contemporary art, architecture, and design. *7380 E. 2nd St., tel. 480/994–2787. $5. Mon.–Sat. 10–5, Thurs. 10–8, Sun. noon–5.*

TEMPE

Charles Trumbell Hayden arrived on the east end of the Salt River in the 1860s. There he built a flour mill and began a ferry service to cross the then-flowing Rio Salado (Salt River), founding the town then known as Hayden's Ferry in 1871. Other settlers soon arrived, including an Englishman who felt—upon approaching the town from Phoenix and seeing the butte, river, and fields of green mesquite—that the name should be changed to Tempe after the Vale of Tempe in Greece. Hayden took umbrage at the suggested name change but finally relented in 1879.

Today Tempe is Arizona's sixth-largest city and the home of Arizona State University's main campus and a thriving student population. A 20-minute drive from Phoenix, the tree- and brick-lined Mill Avenue (on which Hayden's mill still stands) is the main drag, rife with student-oriented hangouts, bookstores, boutiques, eateries, and a repertory movie house.

Tempe's banks of the now-dry Rio Salado are the future site of a sprawling commercial and entertainment district. The ambitious Rio Salado Project will turn the dry Salt River bed into a sprawling leisure, entertainment, and community center. Its first phase, the construction of Tempe Town Lake, was completed in late 1999. The lake, a 2-mi-long waterway created by inflatable dams in a flood control channel, is open for boating for Valley residents, as are new biking and jogging pathways. The project is designed to encourage active recreation and promote development along the river. When completed, Rio Salado will be ringed by parklands, hotels, and restaurants, and will be the largest urban recreation attraction in Arizona.

A Good Walk

Parking is available in the public garage at Hayden Square, just north of 5th Street and west of Mill Avenue. Be sure to have your ticket stamped by local merchants to avoid paying parking fees. The Centerpoint business and shopping center at Mill Avenue and University Drive has a garage that fills quickly. Street parking remains sparse, but the walk along Mill Avenue is a pleasant way to get your bearings. From **La Casa Vieja,** on the southwest corner of Mill Avenue and 1st Street, cross 1st Street and enjoy your stroll through the **Tempe Arts Center** sculpture garden en route to the center itself. Behind the main building, stroll north to the old Mill Avenue bridge where you can check out the Arts Center's rooftop artwork. Turn around and head to the main part of town; walk south on Mill Avenue, passing the old Hayden flour mill, as well as "A" Mountain (decorated by ASU students in school-color gold and protected from raiders from the rival University of Arizona in Tucson). Continue south along shop-lined Mill Avenue until you reach 5th Street; walk a block east on 5th toward the inverted pyramid of **Tempe City Hall.** Follow the pathway west through the grounds of City Hall and Plazita de Descanso, back to Mill Avenue. Head two blocks south on Mill to University Drive and proceed to Gammage Parkway, where you'll find the Grady Gammage Auditorium and ASU art museums and galleries on the southwest corner of the **Arizona State University** campus. You can walk back up Mill Avenue, catch the free FLASH shuttle northward (it stops on the north corner of Gammage Parkway and Mill Avenue, or wind your way northward through the university campus up toward Sun Devil Stadium.

TIMING

If you're planning to shop as well as tour the campus and museums, allow four or five hours for exploring (and periodic breaks) in downtown Tempe.

Sights to See

Arizona State University. What was once the Tempe Normal School for Teachers—in 1886, a four-room redbrick building and 20-acre cow pasture—is now the 750-acre campus of ASU, the largest university in the Southwest. Stop by the **ASU Visitor Information Center** (826 E. Apache Blvd., at Rural Rd., tel. 480/965–0100) for a copy of a self-guided walking tour (it's a long walk from Mill Avenue, so you might opt for the short version suggested here). You'll wind past public art and innovative architecture—including a music building that bears a strong resemblance to a wedding cake (designed by Taliesin students to echo Wright's Gammage Auditorium) and a law library shaped like an open book—and end up at the 74,000-seat **ASU Sun Devil Stadium,** home to the school's Sun Devils and headquarters for the NFL's Arizona Cardinals. Admission to all ASU museums is free.

Heralded for its superior acoustics, the circular **Grady Gammage Auditorium** (Mill Ave. at Apache Blvd., tel. 480/965–4050) was the last public structure completed by architect Frank Lloyd Wright, who detached the rear wall from grand tier and balcony sections in an effort to surround every patron with sound. The stage can accommodate a full symphony orchestra, and there's a 2,909-pipe organ here as well. Artwork is exhibited in the lobby and in two on-site galleries, and free half-hour tours are offered weekdays 1–3:30 during the school year.

While touring the west end of the campus, stop into the gray-purple stucco **Nelson Fine Arts Center** (tel. 480/965–2787), just north of the Gammage Auditorium. The center's museum houses some fine examples of 19th- and 20th-century painting and sculpture by masters such as Winslow Homer, Edward Hopper, Georgia O'Keeffe, and Rockwell Kent; it's an extensive collection for a small museum. You'll also find works by faculty and student artists and an interesting gift shop. *Tues.* 10–9, *Wed.–Sat.* 10–5, *Sun.* 1–5.

A short walk east, just north of the Hayden Library, ASU's experimental gallery and collection of crockery and ceramics are located in the **Matthews Center** (tel. 480/965–2875). *Tues.–Sat.* 10–5. *Closed Jun.–Aug.*

In Matthews Hall, the **Northlight Gallery** (tel. 480/965–6517) exhibits works by both renowned and emerging photographers. *Mon.–Thurs.* 10:30–4:30.

La Casa Vieja. In 1871, when Tempe was still known as Hayden's Ferry, this old house was built as the home of Charles Hayden.

The adobe hacienda is modeled after Spanish mansions and was the town's first building. The late Carl Hayden, former U.S. senator from Arizona, was born here. Now a steak house called Monte's La Casa Vieja, the structure retains its original dimensions; the lobby and dining rooms contain photographs and historical documents pertaining to the frontier history of Tempe. *3 W. 1st St., tel. 480/967–7594. Sun.–Thurs. 11–11, Fri.– Sat. 11 AM–midnight.*

Tempe City Hall. Local architects Rolf Osland and Michael Goodwin constructed this inverted pyramid not just to win design awards (which they have) but also to shield city workers from the desert sun. The pyramid is constructed mainly of bronzed glass and stainless steel; the point disappears in a sunken courtyard lushly landscaped with jacaranda, ivy, and flowers, out of which the pyramid widens to the sky: Stand underneath and gaze up for a weird fish-eye perspective. *31 E. 5th St., 1 block east of Mill Ave., tel. 480/967–2001. Free.*

NEED A BREAK? The outdoor patio of the **Coffee Plantation** (680 S. Mill Ave., tel. 480/829–7878) is a lively scene—students cramming, local residents chatting over a cup of joe, and poets and musicians presenting their latest masterpieces. For a fuller meal, check out **Caffe Boa** (709 S. Mill Ave. tel. 480/968–9112). This friendly spot offers a back courtyard and front patio as well as indoor dining; the upbeat young staff serves creations from panini and crostini to specials like butternut squash soup and seafood ravioli.

In This Chapter

Updated by Cara LaBrie

eating out

ONCE A SLEEPY BACKWATER, the ever-growing Phoenix and its environs draw millions of visitors every year: tourists, conventioneers, and winter snowbirds who roost for months at a time. The population boom has been matched by an astonishing restaurant renaissance. Inventive local chefs have put Southwestern cuisine on the world culinary map, and the native dishes of the area's newer ethnic communities—Persian, Ethiopian, Salvadoran, Vietnamese—have added another dimension to the local palette. Authentic Thai, Chinese, and Indian restaurants are thriving, and there's superb south-of-the-border food from every region of Mexico. Travelers with sophisticated tastes will be thrilled with Phoenix's restaurants, some ranked among the country's best.

Restaurants are remarkably casual. Except for a handful of high-end spots, slacks and sports shirt are dressy enough for men; pants or a simple skirt are appropriate for women.

Remember that restaurants change hours, locations, chefs, prices, and menus frequently, so it's best to call ahead to confirm. Show up without notice during tourist season, and you may find the drive-through window the only place in town without a two-hour wait. All listed restaurants serve dinner and are open for lunch unless otherwise specified.

CATEGORY	COST*
$$$$	over $35
$$$	$26–$35
$$	$15–$25
$	under $15

*per person for a three-course meal, excluding drinks, service, and sales tax

PHOENIX

NORTH CENTRAL PHOENIX
American

$$$ EL CHORRO LODGE. Near the Phoenix Mountains Preserve, El Chorro has been doing business in this picturesque location for 60 years. Sit outside, gaze at the mountains and stars, and try not to make a meal of the famous sticky buns that immediately come to your table. El Chorro's forte is prime-graded meat. Beef Stroganoff, top sirloin, and the chateaubriand for two are tops, and fresh ocean fare such as orange roughy and swordfish are also skillfully prepared. The dense chocolate-chip pecan pie makes dessert a must. 5550 E. Lincoln Dr., tel. 480/948–5170. AE, D, DC, MC, V.

Contemporary

$$$–$$$$ EDDIE MATNEY'S EPICUREAN TRIO. One of Phoenix's top chefs has split with his longtime partner, and is charting a new culinary path on his own. The results are often stunning, occasionally offbeat, and once in a while downright weird. In the fine-dining room, guests with three hours (and $70) to spare can get an eight-course prix-fixe meal. Among the highlights are a wild game consomme, melt-in-your-mouth ahi tuna teamed with Peruvian blue potatoes, beef tenderloin in a high-octane wild mushroom ragout, and a unique take on Boston cream pie. At the less formal bistro, try the fanciful East Meets West Seafood Medley, sesame-crusted ahi over braised bok choy, and Parmesan-crusted sea bass on asparagus risotto. A wine-and-cigar room, available for private parties, completes the "Epicurean Trio." *2398 E. Camelback Rd., tel. 602/957–3214. Reservations essential. AE, D, DC, MC, V. No lunch weekends.*

$$$–$$$$ **ROXSAND.** With a quirky, risky, and imaginative culinary flair,
★ Chef RoxSand Scocos doesn't follow trends; she sets them at one of the most interesting restaurants in the state. Who else would think to stuff tamales with curried lamb moistened in a Thai-style peanut sauce? The heavenly *b'stilla* is a Moroccan-inspired appetizer of braised chicken in phyllo dough, covered with almonds and powdered sugar, and specials such as mango and wild rice soup tap taste buds you didn't know you had. Air-dried duck is an exotic house specialty, served with buckwheat crepes and a pistachio-onion marmalade. Feta-stuffed chicken breast with polenta-fried shrimp is another offbeat success. Desserts are wicked, especially the B-52 torte, an intoxicating disk of chocolate laced with Kahlua and Bailey's. *2594 E. Camelback Rd. (Biltmore Fashion Park), tel. 602/381–0444. Reservations essential. AE, DC, MC, V.*

$$$–$$$$ **T. COOK'S.** This gorgeous place is among the handful of resort
★ restaurants that offer top-of-the-line dining for demanding gastronomes. With its brick walls, painted tile, wooden beams, vaulted ceiling, and marble accents, it looks like an Italianate church. The chef's rustic-Mediterranean fare inspires worshipful devotion, featuring such exquisite delights as grilled lamb loin teamed with wild mushrooms and Swiss chard; herb-rubbed beef tenderloin with Roquefort potato pie; and sea bass wrapped in Parma ham, brightened with olives and artichokes. Civilized portions mean you can indulge freely in dessert. And that's what you'll want to do when you see the massive *collage de chocolat*, a head-turning sampler for two that will have your brain releasing

good-time chemicals for days. *5200 E. Camelback Rd. (Royal Palms), tel. 602/808–0766. Reservations essential. AE, D, DC, MC, V.*

$$$–$$$$ TARBELL'S. Sure it's sleek, smart, and glitzy, but Tarbell's distinguishes itself from the trendoid pack with deftly prepared dishes. The menu changes daily, but you can usually find the vibrant smoked rock shrimp starter. If they're available, order the aromatic mussels, steamed in a heady broth of white wine and shallots. Pricier entrées include a first-rate New York steak with *pommes frites;* on the low end, there's surprisingly good pizza. Your sweet tooth won't be neglected if you opt for the rich Hawaiian chocolate mousse. *3213 E. Camelback Rd., tel. 602/955–8100. Reservations essential. AE, D, DC, MC, V. No lunch.*

$ LON'S AT THE HERMOSA. A beautifully restored 1930s adobe
★ inn with wood-beamed ceilings and beehive fireplaces, Lon's has a rustic Old Arizona feel, but the menu spans the globe. Appetizers may include grilled polenta pie with wild mushroom ragout, ravioli filled with vegetables and goat cheese, or garlic prawns with pineapple relish. Many of the main dishes are grilled over wood: loin of pork, filet mignon, rack of lamb, ahi tuna, and salmon. Pasta, chicken, duck, and veal are other standouts. For dessert, look for the gingered crème brûlée tart or chocolate truffle pâté. *5532 N. Palo Cristi Dr. (Hermosa Inn), tel. 602/955–7878. AE, D, DC, MC, V. No lunch weekends.*

Delicatessen

$–$$ CHOMPIE'S DELI. Run by Brooklyn refugees, this bustling deli with three Valley locations brings a bite of the Big Apple to Phoenix with its smoked fish, blintzes, homemade cream cheeses, and herring in cream sauce. The outstanding bagels will remind New York expats of home—about 20 varieties are baked fresh daily. There's also a top-notch bakery on the premises, with rugalach, pies, and coffee cake. Bring a newspaper, or schmooze with your pals. Sometimes you have to stop and smell the bagels. *3202 E. Greenway Rd., tel. 602/971–8010. Reservations not accepted. AE, MC, V.*

$–$$ MIRACLE MILE DELI. If only cafeteria food were this good in elementary school. This Valley haunt has been a favorite of downtown workers for decades, and the brisket sandwich, piled high, is worth the wait at lunch. Servings are so hefty that table manners sometimes take a back seat. The original location in downtown Phoenix has grown to four restaurants across the Valley. 9 Park Central Mall, tel. 602/277–4783. Reservations not accepted. MC, V. Closed Sun.

French

$$$–$$$$ CHRISTOPHER & PAOLA'S FERMIER BRASSERIE. The Fermier
★ Brasserie—it means, roughly, Farmer's Tavern—may sound rustically informal, but the Gallic-themed fare is strictly big-time. Feather-light ravioli, stuffed with escargots and sweetbreads, start the meal off wonderfully. So does the soup of wild mushrooms and foie gras with a touch of port. Entrées include what may be the best steak dish in town, a prime-grade slab of sirloin, marinated, rubbed with truffles, and lightly smoked. Other main dish favorites include a Provençal-style fish stew, a lovely artichoke tart, and cassoulet. Some of the desserts are so stunning that they've been pictured in national foodie magazines: the chocolate tower and the hot and cold chocolate are two of the best. A terrific by-the-glass wine list and six house-brewed beers add to this restaurant's charms. 2584 E. Camelback Rd. (Biltmore Fashion Park), tel. 602/522–2344. AE, D, DC, MC, V.

$$$ BISTRO 24. Smart and stylish, Bistro 24 beckons diners with its parquet floor, colorful murals, and snazzy bar. Mussels steamed in champagne make a lively first course, and the main dishes tilt toward seafood. Grilled salmon, bouillabaisse, and crispy-skin whitefish are deftly done, as is the steak au poivre, served with French-style frites. Finish up with a soufflé of tart Tatin, and rich French-press coffee. Sunday brunch is outstanding. 2401 E. Camelback Rd. (Ritz-Carlton Hotel), tel. 602/468–0700. AE, D, DC, MC, V.

Greek

$$–$$$ GREEKFEST. This pretty place with whitewashed walls feels like an island taverna and brings the flavors of the Aegean to life. Among the appetizers, look for *taramosalata* (mullet roe blended with lemon and olive oil) and *saganaki* (*kefalograviera* cheese flamed with brandy and extinguished with a squirt of lemon). Entrées, many featuring lamb and shrimp, are equally hard-hitting. Try *exohiko* (chunks of lamb mixed with eggplant, peppers, zucchini, and mushrooms). For dessert, the *galaktoboureko* (warm custard pie baked in phyllo dough and scented with cloves and honey) is a triumph of Western civilization. 1940 E. Camelback Rd., tel. 602/265–2990. AE, D, DC, MC, V. No lunch Sun.

Indian

$$ TASTE OF INDIA. Bread is one of the tests of an Indian kitchen, and the models here—*bhatura*, nan, *paratha*, *poori*—are superb. Just about every spice in the rack is used for such dishes as lamb *kashmiry* and tandoori chicken. Vegetarians will enjoy this spot's wonderful meatless specialties, including *benghan bhartha*, fashioned from eggplant, or *bhindi masala*, a tempting okra dish. Indian desserts include fragrant *ras malai*, a Bengali treat of sweet milk and cheese, with bits of pistachio. 1609 E. Bell Rd., tel. 602/788–3190. AE, D, MC, V.

Italian

$$–$$$$ IL FORNO. This is one of the nicest-looking places in town with cherry wood, sleek, shiny mirrors, and eye-catching prints, and the contemporary Italian fare is just as attractive. Chicken breast stuffed with wild mushrooms, figs, and plums, moistened by a sweet white wine sauce, is one of the town's best entrées. Rack of lamb and the seafood stew in a lobster and white wine broth both shine. So does the *pappardelle alla Bolognese*, wide pasta ribbons bathed in a dreamy veal sauce. In a town bursting with

Italian restaurants, Il Forno is one of only a handful of standouts. 4225 E. Camelback Rd., tel. 602/952–1522. AE, MC, V. No lunch.

$$–$$$ CHRISTO'S RISTORANTE. Small and unassuming in a Phoenix strip mall, Christo's keeps its tables filled with loyal customers lunch and dinner. Attentive servers ensure your glass never empties and bread doesn't have enough time to cool. Entrées come with delicious soup and salad—a meal in their own right—and the flavorful wine sauces will make you wish for a recipe. For dessert, the light tiramisu literally melts in your mouth. 6327 N. 7th St., tel. 602/264–1784. AE, D, DC, MC, V. Closed Sun.

Latin

$$–$$$ HAVANA PATIO CAFE. This Cuban and Latin-American restaurant says "Yanqui, come back" with its flavorful but not too spicy fare. Appetizers are marvelous, particularly the shrimp pancakes, potato croquettes, and Cuban tamale. The best main dishes are the *ropa vieja*, shredded braised beef served with *moros*, a blend of black beans and rice; *pollo Cubano*, chicken breast marinated in lime, orange, and garlic; and *mariscos con salsa verde*, shellfish simmered in a traditional green sauce. Vegetarians will adore the *causa azulada*, a Peruvian platter featuring a blue mashed-potato cake layered with carrot and served on Swiss chard. 6245 E. Bell Rd., tel. 480/991–1496. AE, D, DC, MC, V.

Mexican

$$ RICHARDSON'S. This neighborhood haunt can be noisy and the waitstaff surly, but the fiery fugue of flavors known as New Mexican–style still packs 'em in until midnight. Loose-cushioned, adobe booths surround three sides of a lively bar, and an open kitchen turns out chiles relleno, enchiladas, and other first-rate standbys. Shrimp, chicken, and chops come off the pecan wood-burning grill with distinctive, savory undertones; Chimayo chicken is flavorfully stuffed with spinach, dried tomatoes, poblano chilies, and asiago cheese, and served with a twice-baked green chile potato. There's a wait on weekends, so don't expect to linger at the table after dinner. 1582 E. Bethany Home Rd., tel. 602/265–5886. AE, MC, V.

$ BLUE BURRITO GRILLE. "Healthy Mexican food" used to be an oxymoron, but not anymore. Here you can find good-for-you, south-of-the-border fare without the lard but with all the taste. Among the heart-healthy menu items are chicken burritos, fish tacos, tamales Mexicanos, enchiladas rancheras, vegetarian burritos, and outstanding blue corn vegetarian tacos. 3118 E. Camelback Rd., tel. 602/955–9596. Reservations not accepted. AE, MC, V.

$ EL BRAVO. The decor here consists of the collage of bad checks
★ posted by the "Order Here" window. But cognoscenti of Mexican food won't care about the decorating lapses; they come for the town's best Sonoran fare. (Sonora is the Mexican state that borders Arizona.) Burros here are edible works of art, like the *machaca* (shredded beef) *burro.* Enchiladas, chimichangas, and tacos are just as thrilling. If you've got a taste for chile zest, try the red beef popover—it will leave your tongue tingling. Even the sweets are outstanding. Go for the chocolate chimichanga—it's like a creamy Mexican s'more. 8338 N. 7th St., tel. 602/943–9753. Reservations not accepted. MC, V.

Southwestern

$$$–$$$$ VINCENT GUERITHAULT ON CAMELBACK. It's hard to tell whether
★ Chef Guerithault prepares French food with a Southwestern flair, or Southwestern fare with a French touch. But whatever this talented chef prepares will be incredibly tempting. Make a meal of the famous appetizers: the duck tamale, smoked salmon quesadilla, and chipotle lobster ravioli are all ravishing. Main dishes are just as strong. The duck confit, rack of lamb, and grilled wild boar loin make choosing difficult, and the sautéed veal sweetbreads with blue cornmeal are out-of-this-world. The signature crème brûlée arrives in three thin pastry cups filled with vanilla, coffee, and coconut

custard. *3930 E. Camelback Rd., tel. 602/224–0225. Reservations essential. AE, D, DC, MC, V. No lunch weekends.*

$$ **SAM'S CAFE.** This is the Southwestern restaurant that locals bring their skittish Midwestern relatives to with perfect confidence. Nothing's too far out, but most everything is interesting and tasty. The fragrant poblano chicken chowder is fine, as are the Sedona spring rolls, flour tortillas wrapped around chicken and veggies, with a chipotle barbecue sauce. The hands-down main-dish winner is the inventive chicken-fried tuna, a lightly battered slab adorned with a jalapeño cream gravy, served with chile-mashed potatoes. Steaks, chops, tacos, and pastas (try the chicken pasta, flamed with tequila) are outstanding, and the chilled flan, fashioned from yams, drizzled with caramel sauce, and garnished with pecans, is worth a dessert splurge. *2566 E. Camelback Rd. (Biltmore Fashion Park), tel. 602/954–7100. AE, D, DC, MC, V.*

Spanish

$$–$$$ **ALTOS.** This hot spot attracts sophisticated locals who bask in the scents of Iberia—garlic, sherry, olive oil, saffron. Calamari de Pedro (tender squid dipped in a saffron batter and sizzled in olive oil) is a good appetizer for sharing. *Sombrilla Andaluza* is mesmerizing, a Portobello mushroom marinated in olive oil, garlic, and sherry, then grilled and festooned with red cabbage, parsley, and Serrano ham. Main dishes are also invigorating. The *filete pelon* is a buttery filet mignon topped with cabrales, a creamy Spanish blue cheese. *Lomo en adobo* is pork loin smothered in a lusty sauce with hints of chile, sesame seeds, sugar, and peanuts. The sugar-glazed chocolate espresso crème brûlée may be the single best dessert in Arizona. *5029 N. 44th St., tel. 602/808–0890. AE, D, DC, MC, V. No lunch weekends.*

Steak

$$$–$$$$ **MORTON'S.** This national chain doesn't stint on quality and doesn't believe in menus: you have to sit through a 10-minute recital by your server to find out what's served. The New York sirloin is what beef is all about, a ravishing 20-ounce strip that perfectly packages looks, taste, and texture, and the juicy 24-ounce porterhouse is heart-stopping. The à la carte side dishes are big enough to split two or three ways, but if you have room for dessert try the chocolate Godiva cake, a moist sponge cake with a molten chocolate interior. 2425 E. Camelback Rd. (Shops at the Esplanade), tel. 602/955–9577. AE, DC, MC, V. No lunch.

$$ TEXAZ GRILL. The down-home fare here is served in a cowboy setting that oozes with neighborhood charm. The T-bone steak and butter-soft fillet are very satisfying, but it's the he-man-size chicken-fried steak that lures most folks here. The fork-tender beef is encased in crisp batter and ladled with thick, peppery country gravy; the mashed potato side—with the skin mashed in—is a worthy accompaniment. Order yourself a Lone Star brew, put some coins in the jukebox, and loosen your belt. 6003 N. 16th St., tel. 602/248–7827. Reservations not accepted. AE, MC, V. No lunch Sun.

CENTRAL PHOENIX
American

$–$$ CORONADO CAFÉ. You might miss this hidden treasure if it weren't for the lines of customers waiting outside at lunchtime. This charming 1950s residence in the heart of Phoenix has merely 30 seats and immediate parking for three vehicles, but there's always room for homemade favorites such as chicken corn chowder (with huge chunks of potato) or a chicken Caesar sandwich you'll need a fork to eat. The entrées change daily, but on a hot summer day, be sure to order the homemade tea (it's BYOB if you desire something with a little more kick). 2201 N. 7th St., tel. 602/258–5149. Reservations not accepted. MC, V. Closed Sun.–Mon. No dinner Sat.

Barbecue

$ HONEY BEAR'S BBQ. Honey Bear's motto—"You don't need no teeth to eat our meat"—may fall short on grammar, but this place isn't packed with folks looking to improve their language skills. If you've got barbecue fever, the meaty pork ribs are the cure. This is Tennessee-style barbecue, which means smoky baby backs basted in thick, zippy, slightly sweet sauce with a wonderful orange tang. The sausage-enhanced "cowbro" beans and scallion-studded potato salad are great sides. If a slab of ribs still leaves you hungry, finish up with the homemade sweet potato pie. 5012 E. Van Buren St., tel. 602/273–9148. Reservations not accepted. AE, D, MC, V.

Chinese

$–$$ GOURMET HOUSE OF HONG KONG. This popular Chinese restaurant draws customers who are interested in genuine Chinatown specialties like chow fun (thick rice noodles). Try the assorted meat version, topped with chicken, shrimp, pork, and squid. Lobster with black bean sauce may be the world's messiest platter, but it's also one of the tastiest. Don't wear anything that needs to be dry-cleaned. Along with an extensive seafood list, such adventurous delights as five-flavor frogs' legs, duck feet with greens, and beef tripe casserole are offered. 1438 E. McDowell Rd., tel. 602/253–4859. AE, D, DC, MC, V.

French

$$$ COUP DES TARTES. This cozy, casual, wonderfully homey, BYOB
★ spot—it used to be an antiques store—serves deftly crafted Mediterranean-accented fare. Start off with a charcuterie platter, and move on to delightful main-course fare like fennel-tinged sea bass, ginger-spiked pork tenderloin, and the house specialty, braised lamb shank with couscous. The chef-proprietor trained as pastry chef, and her signature dessert tarts show she's been well taught. The banana-brulée tart is especially marvelous. 4626 N. 16th St., tel. 602/212–1082. Reservations essential. AE, D, DC, MC, V. Closed Sun.–Mon. No lunch.

Italian

$$–$$$ **LA FONTANELLA.** This outstanding neighborhood Italian restaurant
★ is a winning combination of quality and value. The mom-and-pop
proprietors deliver all the hard-hitting flavors of their native land:
suppli, a Roman specialty, rice croquettes filled with cheese; and
escargots, bubbling in garlic and butter, get the meal off to a fast
start. All the entrées are first-rate; some are out-of-this-world.
Among the latter are lamb *agrassato,* lamb shank braised in wine
with raisins, pine nuts, and potatoes; osso buco, gilded with
pancetta; seafood *reale,* shrimp and scallops in a sherry cream
sauce; and the herb-crusted rack of lamb. For dessert, La
Fontanella's homemade gelato puts an exclamation mark on
dinner. *4231 E. Indian School Rd., tel. 602/955–1213. AE, D, DC, MC,
V. No lunch weekends.*

Latin

$ **ELIANA'S RESTAURANT.** This simple, family-run gem features
budget-priced El Salvadoran specialties skillfully prepared. You
can make a meal of the appetizers: *pupusas* (corn patties stuffed
with pork, peppers, and cheese); *pasteles* (meat turnovers); and
tamales, filled with chicken and vegetables. Main dishes will
wipe out hunger pangs for about the price of a movie ticket.
There's *pollo encebollado* (fried chicken with rice and beans), and
mojarra frita, a whole fried tilapia, an Arizona farm-raised fish
popular in Latin America. You can wash your meal down with
refreshing homemade fruit drinks. *1627 N. 24th St., tel. 602/225–
2925. Reservations not accepted. AE, D, MC, V. Closed Mon.*

Mexican

$$–$$$ **NORMAN'S ARIZONA.** Chef Norman Fierros' scintillating "Nueva
Mexicana" cuisine is aimed at sophisticated locals tired of gringo
combination-plate fare. Start off with scrumptious *tamalitos,* baby
tamales made from vigorous red chilies or sweet green corn.

Appetizer salads are also superb, especially the endives tossed with Mexican cheese and roasted pecans. Main dishes are highly energetic, like the chile mash: mashed spuds capped by a poblano chile and surrounded by morsels of chicken in mole. Steak picado, rabbit in a spicy red chile marinade, and grilled sea bass with *culiche* (a squash-and-corn mix) also hit the mark. And no one does south-of-the-border desserts like Norman. His creamy chocolate chimichangas and fabulous banana squash pie are almost legendary. *4410 N. 40th St., tel. 602/956–2288. AE, D, MC, V. Closed Mon. No lunch weekends.*

$$–$$$ **SUCH IS LIFE.** No gringo touches here: authentic, Yucatan-
★ inspired Mexican fare keeps the place packed. For starters, try the *nopal polanco*, a prickly pear cactus pad topped with Chihuahua cheese and chorizo. The lusty, lemon-tinged chicken soup is also thick with poultry, avocado, and hard-boiled egg. Entrées include chicken mole and adobo pork, simmered in a fragrant ancho chile, sesame-orange sauce. If the kitchen has Gulf shrimp, get them grilled in garlic. *3602 N. 24th St., tel. 602/955–7822. Reservations essential. AE, D, DC, MC, V. Closed Sun. No lunch Sat.*

$$ **SAN CARLOS BAY SEAFOOD RESTAURANT.** From the street, San
★ Carlos Bay doesn't look like much, but the best Mexican seafood in town is served inside. Start off with a seafood cocktail teeming with octopus or shrimp, in a riveting tomato-based liquid spiked with onions, cilantro, lime, and pepper. Among the main dishes, the Veracruz-style filleted snapper is coated with olives, onions, tomatoes, and peppers. The delicious, meaty crustaceans come soaked in a devilishly hot sauce. For seafood that doesn't make your nostrils flare, try the well-stocked seven seas stew. *1901 E. McDowell Rd., tel. 602/340–0892. Reservations not accepted. No credit cards.*

$–$$ **LOS DOS MOLINOS.** Is this the place that launched a thousand
★ chips? You bet it is. This restaurant features New Mexican–style Mexican food. For the uninitiated, that means HOT!—you'll know

after one bite. Legions of heat seekers practically worship the Hatch, New Mexico chilies that form the backbone of the dishes here. Adobada ribs, a specialty, feature fall-off-the-bone meat marinated in red chilies, and the green chile enchilada and beef taco are potentially lethal. But there's flavor in this fire. The sopaipilla, a pillow of fried dough doused with cinnamon, honey, or powdered sugar, is the New Mexican antidote to chile flames, but if you can't stand the heat, stay out of this kitchen. 8646 S. Central Ave., tel. 602/243–9113. Reservations not accepted. AE, D, MC, V. Closed Sun.–Mon.

Pizza

$–$$ PIZZERIA BIANCO. Bronx-native Chris Bianco makes pizza good ★ enough to inspire memories of Naples, even if you've never been there. The secret? A wood-fired brick oven and a passion for quality. Bianco's pizza crust is a work of art, not too bready, not too light, and just chewy enough to keep your jaws happy. Toppings include imported cheeses, homemade fennel sausage, wood-roasted cremini mushrooms, and the freshest herbs and spices. There are also antipasto and sandwiches on fresh-baked bread. 623 E. Adams St., tel. 602/258–8300. MC, V. Closed Mon. No lunch weekends.

Seafood

$$ STEAMED BLUES. Crabs in the desert? No, it's not a mirage. This restaurant specializes in blue crabs that are still swimming when you order them. Prepare for the din of pounding mallets as diners attack their dinner—you might think you're in the middle of the "Anvil Chorus" scene in "Il Trovatore." If you prefer not to hammer your meal, there are soft-shell crabs, as well as crab cakes and steamed shrimp. The "Boardwalk" fries—fresh-cut, seasoned, sizzling potatoes—will make you think you're near the ocean. 4843 N. 8th Pl., tel. 480/966–2722. Reservations not accepted. AE, D, DC, MC, V. No lunch weekends.

Steak

$$ T-BONE STEAK HOUSE. You won...
dances at T-Bone Steak House...
steaks in a ranch-house setting. T...
a monstrous 2-pound porterh...
ounce sirloin, all of them juicy...
view. The restaurant sits about...
at dusk for a great look at the...
S. 19th Ave., tel. 602/276–0945. *Reservations* not...
MC, V. No lunch.

SCOTTSDALE

American

$$$$ **TERRACE DINING ROOM.** The Phoenician's Terrace Dining Room
★ serves the most lavish (and expensive) Sunday brunch in town.
Attention is paid to every detail, from the wheel of costly Parmesan-
Reggiano cheese to the fresh artichoke hearts in the salad. First,
wander around the sushi section, the jumbo shrimp table, the
homemade pastas, the pâtés, the crepes, and the blintzes and
waffles. Then stroll to the main dishes: salmon and lamb chops
are fired up on the grill, and filet mignon and pork tenderloin in
port sauce are warmed in trays. Save room for such desserts as
homemade ice cream, elegant chocolate truffles, or pear-rhubarb
tart. Champagne keeps the meal bubbling, so don't plan anything
more strenuous than a nap for the afternoon. *6000 E. Camelback
Rd. (The Phoenician), tel. 480/423–2530. Reservations essential. AE, D,
DC, MC, V.*

$$$–$$$$ **THE GRILL AT THE TPC.** Everything is way over par at The Grill:
this clubhouse grill is one of the best restaurants in town, but it's
not for thrill-seeking foodies after great adventures in modern
gastronomy. It is the place for prime steaks, both dry-aged and
wet-aged beef, and stunning seafood, flown in fresh daily. For proof,

...use-smoked shark special or phenomenal sesame-
...ahi tuna. Even nonsmokers will be happy to conclude their
... with a cigar and matchbox made of white chocolate. 7575
...Princess Dr. (Scottsdale Princess Resort), tel. 480/585–4848. Reservations
essential. AE, D, DC, MC, V.

$$ **GOLDEN SWAN.** This desert oasis is a great place for a leisurely
Sunday champagne brunch. Sit outside under umbrellas or in a
covered pavilion that juts into a koi-filled lagoon ringed by palms
and hibiscus. The Golden Swan has a unique brunch shtick:
everything except dessert is laid out in the kitchen under the
watchful eyes of toque-clad chefs. Try the veal tortellini in lobster
sauce, giant prawns, or filet mignon. 7500 E. Doubletree Ranch Rd.
(Hyatt Regency at Gainey Ranch), tel. 480/991–3388. Reservations
essential. AE, D, DC, MC, V.

American/Casual

$–$$ **BANDERA.** If you're looking for a quick, tasty dinner before a night
out on the town, try this casual, high-volume spot. The weekly menu
includes wonderfully moist and meaty rotisserie chicken; you'll
see the birds spinning in the big window before you even walk
through the door. If you're not a poultry fan, salads, fresh fish,
prime rib, and meat loaf usually make it on the menu. The mashed
potatoes are divine—you'll think Mom is in the kitchen peeling
spuds. If you get here at prime eating hours, especially on
weekends, be prepared to wait for a table. 3821 N. Scottsdale Rd.,
tel. 480/994–3524. Reservations not accepted. AE, MC, V. No lunch.

$ **ORIGINAL PANCAKE HOUSE.** This breakfast landmark does one
thing—pancakes—and does it extremely well. These flapjacks
inspire worship from local admirers who wait patiently for a table
on weekends. Chief among the griddled glories is the signature
apple pancake: Homemade batter is poured over sautéed apples
and partially baked. Then the concoction is flipped over, glazed
with cinnamon sugar and baked some more. It's creamy, sweet,
bubbly . . . and huge. Other varieties, like the German pancake,

are also exceptional. *6840 E. Camelback Rd., tel. 480/946–4902. Reservations not accepted. No credit cards.*

Contemporary

$$$–$$$$ MICHAEL'S AT THE CITADEL. One of this town's best-looking places (check out the brick-lined waterfall at the entrance), Michael's contemporary American fare is as elegant as the setting. The entrées are the real stars here: pan-seared duck paired with foie gras and pearl couscous; sesame-crusted swordfish with green coconut curry; venison with a dried-cherry demiglace; grilled lamb with a goat-cheese potato tart. If you're celebrating a special occasion, Michael's is the spot. *8700 E. Pinnacle Peak Rd., tel. 480/515–2575. AE, DC, MC, V.*

$$$–$$$$ ★ RANCHO PINOT GRILL. The attention to quality paid by the husband-and-wife proprietors here—he manages, she cooks— has made this one of the town's top eating spots. The inventive menu changes daily, depending on what's fresh. If you're lucky, you might come on a day when the kitchen features *posole*, a mouthwatering broth with hominy, salt pork, and cabbage. Entrées include quail with soba noodles, rosemary-infused chicken with Italian sausage, and grilled sea bass atop basmati rice. *6208 N. Scottsdale Rd., tel. 602/468–9463. Reservations essential. AE, D, MC, V. Closed Sun.–Mon. and mid-Aug.–mid-Sept. No lunch.*

$$$ COWBOY CIAO. Looking for a culinary kick? This kitchen weds Southwestern fare and Italian flair, and it's no shotgun wedding, either. Main dishes, like the Chianti-marinated filet mignon, fennel-seasoned meat loaf, and wild mushrooms in an ancho chile cream sauce heaped over polenta, are creative without going off the deep end. The chocolate lottery—complete with an actual lottery ticket—is a dessert hoot. The imaginative wine list has affordable flights that let you taste several wines with your meal. *7133 E. Stetson Dr., tel. 480/946–3111. AE, D, DC, MC, V. No lunch Sun.–Mon.*

phoenix and scottsdale dining

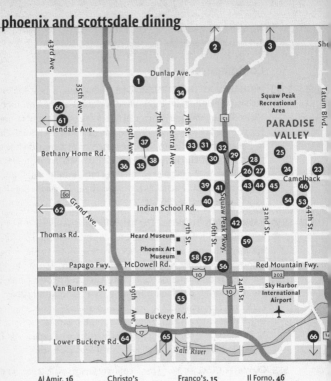

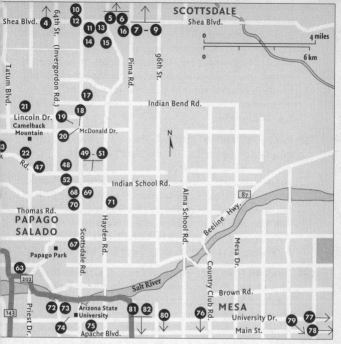

$$$ GREGORY'S GRILL. This charming bistro is tiny, with seating for
★ maybe 40 patrons. The menu is equally small, but outstanding.
Look for appetizers such as duck prosciutto, salmon seviche, and
a lovely tower fashioned from veggies and goat cheese. Entrées
include beer-marinated beef tenderloin, apple-crusted salmon,
and grilled pork chops with quinoa risotto. Note: You can save a
bundle by bringing your own beer or wine. 7049 E. McDowell Rd.
(Papago Plaza shopping center), tel. 480/946–8700. AE, D, MC, V. Closed
Sun.–Mon. No lunch.

$$$ RAZZ'S RESTAURANT AND BAR. There's no telling what part of
the globe chef-proprietor Erasmo "Razz" Kamnitzer will use for
culinary inspiration. However, you can count on his creations to
give dormant taste buds a wake-up call: black bean paella is a twist
on a Spanish theme; South American bouillabaisse is a fragrant
fish stew, stocked with veggies; and *bah mie goreng* teams noodles
with fish, meat, and vegetables, perked up with dried cranberries
and almonds. Count on it—Razz'll dazzle. 10321 N. Scottsdale Rd.,
tel. 480/905–1308. AE, D, DC, MC, V. Closed Sun.–Mon. No lunch.

$$$ ROARING FORK. The restaurant's name is supposed to reflect
what the chef calls "Western American cuisine." It means appetizers
like the cornmeal crepe, stuffed with Portobello mushrooms and
coated in red pepper sauce, or the smashing cracked-corn stuffing,
teamed with turkey confit and dried figs. Two particularly
outstanding entrées are skillet-seared pompano, embellished
with crawfish and smoked ham hock, and riveting sugar-and-chile-
cured duck, served with green chile macaroni. The dessert highlight
is the tart Tatin, here made with pears, not apples, and goosed
up with a vigorous ginger snap. 7243 E. Camelback Rd., tel. 480/947–
0795. AE, D, DC, MC, V. Closed Sun. No lunch.

$$ L'ECOLE. You'll have no regrets putting yourself in the talented
hands of the student-chefs at the Valley's premier cooking
academy. You get a three-course dinner for about $20, a real
bargain. Look for inventive appetizers like ginger soy gravlax,

and main dishes like fillet Rossini. Because the students also pull server duty, you can count on being pampered, too. 8100 E. Camelback Rd. (Scottsdale Culinary Institute), tel. 480/990–7639. Reservations essential. D, MC, V. Closed weekends.

French

$$$$ MARY ELAINE'S. Swanky, formal, and austerely elegant, this is the Phoenician's showcase restaurant, with big picture windows commanding a sweeping view of Phoenix. The French/Mediterranean menu leads with starters such as calamari and cuttlefish gazpacho and foie gras with caramelized kumquats, then reveals the chef's way with fish. Entrées include monkfish medallions in orange-Burgundy sauce, turbot with fresh hearts of palm, and John Dory accented with fennel. A superb wine list enhances the meal, which might close with nougat glacé with candied grapefruit and Tahitian vanilla sauce. 6000 E. Camelback Rd. (The Phoenician), tel. 480/941–8200. Reservations essential. Jacket required. AE, D, DC, MC, V. Closed Sun. No lunch.

Italian

$$$–$$$$ FRANCO'S TRATTORIA. The Florence-born Franco puts together
★ meals that sing with the flavors of Tuscany. Start with focaccia and hunks of imported Italian cheeses sliced off huge wheels. Next, sample the antipasto or the tasty risotto. Main dishes are hearty and vibrant; naturally, veal is a specialty: the orecchie d'elefante (so named because it seems as massive as an elephant's ear) is pounded to millimeter thinness, breaded, fried, and splayed across the plate, coated with tomatoes and shallots, basil, and lemon. 8120 N. Hayden Rd., tel. 480/948–6655. AE, MC, V. Closed Sun. and July. No lunch.

$$$–$$$$ LECCABAFFI RISTORANTE. Leccabaffi means "lick the mustache," and that's what you'll want to do after scraping these plates clean. The temptation begins just inside the entrance, where an antipasto table groans with grilled and roasted vegetables. The stars here are the lusty northern Italian meat, fish, and poultry dishes. The *Costoletta alla Valdostana* (a bone-in veal chop with a pocket of fontina cheese) is a triumph. The wine-soaked quail, filet mignon in a Gorgonzola sauce, and Roman-style semolina gnocchi also shine. Finish up with a glass of sweet *vin santo*, Tuscany's classic dessert wine, and a house-made biscottilife is good. *9719 N. Hayden Rd., tel. 480/609–0429. AE, D, MC, V. Closed Mon. No lunch.*

\$\$–\$\$\$ MARIA'S WHEN IN NAPLES. In a town teeming with Italian restaurants, this is a standout. The antipasto spread laid out just inside the entrance is sure to grab your attention, and it tastes as good as it looks. The homemade pasta is another winner. Check out the *salsiccia Pugliese* (fettuccine topped with homemade sausage, leeks, porcini mushrooms, and white wine sauce), or the *orecchiette Barese* (ear-shape pasta tossed with cauliflower, pancetta, sun-dried tomatoes, olive oil, and cheese). *7000 E. Shea Blvd., tel. 480/991–6887. AE, D, DC, MC, V. No lunch weekends.*

\$ OREGANO'S. This happening, jam-packed pizza-pasta-sandwich parlor lures customers with two irresistible come-ons: good food and low prices. Oregano's offers two types of Chicago pizza: stuffed deep-dish and thin-crust, and both are great. So are the untraditional lasagna, particularly the artichoke one, made with whole-wheat pasta (it's worth the 30-minute wait). Sandwich fans will appreciate the baked Italian hoagie, stuffed with pepperoni, capicolla, salami, and provolone, then loaded with tomatoes, onions, peppers, and olives. This original location was such a hit that two other Valley Oregano's have opened. *3622 N. Scottsdale Rd., tel. 480/970–1860. Reservations not accepted. AE, D, MC, V.*

Japanese

\$\$–\$\$\$ SUSHI ON SHEA. You may be in the middle of the desert, but the sushi here will make you think you're at the ocean's edge. Yellowtail, toro, shrimp, scallops, freshwater eel, and even

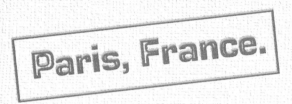

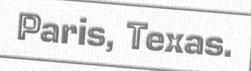

When it Comes to Getting Cash at an ATM,

Same Thing.

Whether you're in Yosemite or Yemen, using your Visa® card or ATM card with the PLUS symbol is the easiest and most convenient way to get cash. Even if your bank is in Minneapolis and you're in Miami, Visa/PLUS ATMs make getting cash so easy, you'll feel right at home. After all, Visa/PLUS ATMs are open 24 hours a day, 7 days a week, rain or shine. And if you need help finding one of Visa's 627,000 ATMs in 127 countries worldwide, visit **visa.com/pd/atm**. We'll make finding an ATM as easy as finding the Eiffel Tower, the Pyramids or even the Grand Canyon.

It's Everywhere You Want To Be.

monkfish liver pâté are among the long list of delights here. Check out the *nabemono* (hot pot or meals-in-a-bowl) prepared at your table. The best dish? Maybe it's the *una-ju* (broiled freshwater eel with a sublime smoky scent), served over sweet rice. The fact that some people believe eel is an aphrodisiac only adds to its charm. *7000 E. Shea Blvd., tel. 480/483–7799. AE, D, DC, MC, V. No lunch.*

Mexican

$$$ LA HACIENDA. The food here is nothing like the run-from-the-
★ border fare you find at neighborhood taco stands—it's more like the food of Mexico's colonial grandee. The appetizers, such as a mushroom crepe enlivened with *huitlacoche* (a fungus of almost trufflelike intensity), are stunning. The entrées are heavy with seafood: huge, grilled Gulf shrimp; red snapper in a Veracruzana sauce; seared tuna, crusted with wheat flour and served with a roasted poblano and caramelized onion cake. *Cochinillo asado* is La Hacienda's signature dish—roast suckling pig, wheeled up to the table and carved to order. Finish with *cajeta* ice-cream crepes or the mesmerizing pumpkin-chocolate cheesecake. *7575 E. Princess Dr. (Scottsdale Princess Resort), tel. 480/585–4848. AE, D, DC, MC, V. No lunch.*

$–$$ CARLSBAD TAVERN. This is Mexican food served New Mexican style, which means dishes with a hot-chile bite. Get yourself a potent frozen margarita (there's a nice selection of premium tequilas) to wash down starters like red chile potato pancakes and ravioli stuffed with smoked duck and tequila-marinated grilled shrimp. Entrées continue the flavor assault: *carne adovada* is pork simmered in red chile sauce; the *machaca* tamale duo features two shredded beef tamales, one in green chile sauce, the other coated with spicy red chile; and lamb pierna, a wood-grilled, braised leg of lamb topped with red wine sauce. *3313 N. Hayden Rd., tel. 480/970–8156. AE, D, MC, V.*

Middle Eastern

$–$$ AL AMIR. Along with traditional appetizer favorites like *baba ghanouj* (mashed eggplant), hummus, falafel, and tabbouleh, this spot serves *ma'anek*, juicy Lebanese sausages zinged with cloves, and *safiha*, canape-size pockets of dough stuffed with ground lamb. Main dishes feature kabobs, but it pays to explore the less familiar options. The *kebbe bil sanyeh* is sensational with layers of heavily seasoned ground beef baked with bulgur wheat and pine nuts. Don't leave without ordering *knafeh*, a warm cheese pastry smothered in syrup. *8989 E. Via Linda, tel. 480/661–1137. AE, D, MC, V. Closed Sun.*

Pan-Asian

$$$ RESTAURANT HAPA. "Hapa" is Hawaiian slang for "half," which
★ describes the half-Japanese, half-American background of the chef. But there's nothing halfway about Hapa's astonishingly flavorful, Asian-inspired cuisine. Appetizers such as skillet-roasted mussels coated in a Thai-inspired broth scented with lemongrass, mint, basil, ginger, and coconut let you know you're in for a big-time experience. The signature entrée is beef tenderloin, lined with hot Chinese mustard and caramelized brown sugar. Desserts are just as inspired as the other courses: look for the skillet of Asian pears with a macadamia-nut crust and Saigon cinnamon ice cream, or the coconut crème brûlée tart. *6204 N. Scottsdale Rd., tel. 480/998–8220. AE, MC, V. Closed Sun. No lunch.*

$$$ ROY'S. Roy Yamaguchi, a James Beard award–winning chef and one of the pioneers of Pacific Rim cooking, has restaurants scattered all over the globe. Look for inventive dishes like steamed pork and crab buns with a spicy Maui onion black bean sauce; lemongrass tempura chicken breast; tiger prawns on a lobster Alfredo sauce; and nori-crusted ono with a hot and sour red pepper sauce. It's sophisticated food for sophisticated palates. *7001 N. Scottsdale Rd. (Scottsdale Seville), tel. 480/905–1155. AE, MC, V. No lunch.*

Seafood

$$$–$$$$ **RESTAURANT OCEANA.** When you're 400 mi from the nearest ocean, you can expect to pay for your seafood thrills. You'll pay at Restaurant Oceana, but you'll also get plenty of thrills. Everything here was swimming in the sea 24 hours ago. The daily-changing menu may include scallops the size of hockey pucks, Casco Bay cod, Belon oysters from Washington, and mahimahi. Bing cherry shortcake with honey whipped cream, jasmine rice pudding with pineapple soup, and chocolate cake with a molten chocolate center are just three of the can't-miss desserts. *8900 E. Pinnacle Peak Rd., tel. 480/515–2277. AE, D, DC, MC, V. Closed Sun. No lunch.*

Southwestern

$$$ **CAFE TERRA COTTA.** This Scottsdale branch of the acclaimed
★ Tucson original shows you how the Southwest was won using inventive regional creations and sophisticated flavors. Start off with buffalo carpaccio drizzled with chile-infused oil or a quesadilla filled with duck and smoked Gouda cheese. Next, move to lamb chops in an ancho-chile *mole* (pronounced *mo-lay,* this is a spicy chocolate-and-nut-based sauce) or salmon crusted with sunflower seeds and yellow chile sauce. Desserts are just as formidable, especially the orange-curd tart. *6166 N. Scottsdale Rd. (Borgata Shopping Center), tel. 480/948–8100. AE, D, DC, MC, V.*

Spanish

$$$–$$$$ **MARQUESA.** This gem of a restaurant pays homage to Catalonia,
★ the region around Barcelona. Everything here is right on target, from the setting to the service. Appetizers are extraordinary: *anec d'Napoleon,* phyllo dough pouches stuffed with a heady blend of duck, foie gras, and mushrooms; and *pebrots del piquillo,* crab and fontina cheese baked into sweet red peppers. Main dishes include monkfish-veal loin duo; pan-roasted rack of lamb; and a first-class paella crammed with lobster, shrimp, mussels, clams, chicken, and *chistora* (a sharp Spanish sausage). For dessert, the Gran

Torres cheesecake and flan are equally wonderful. 7575 E. Princess Dr. (Scottsdale Princess Resort), tel. 480/585–4848. Reservations essential. AE, D, DC, MC, V. No lunch.

Steak

$$$ DON & CHARLIE'S. A favorite with major-leaguers in town for spring training, this venerable chophouse specializes in prime-grade steak and baseball memorabilia—the walls are covered with pictures, autographs, and uniforms. The New York sirloin, prime rib, and double-thick lamb chops are a hit; sides include au gratin potatoes and creamed spinach. Serious carnivores will not strike out here. 7501 E. Camelback Rd., tel. 480/990–0900. AE, D, DC, MC, V. No lunch.

$–$$ PINNACLE PEAK PATIO. This spot is strictly for tourists, but it's no trap. More than 1,600 diners can sit inside this Western restaurant, the largest in the world; another 1,400 can dine under the stars out on the patio. Founded in 1957, the Peak hasn't altered its menu in years—a menu that consists solely of five grilled steaks and hickory-roasted chicken. "Big Marv" Dickson has personally manned the grill since 1961, cooking up more than 2 million pounds of beef himself—he credits delectable porterhouse and T-bones to mesquite smoke's magic, but everyone else knows Marv as a Steak Jedi, with a sixth sense for beef. Country bands play nightly. Wear a tie you don't mind leaving behind. 10426 E. Jomax Rd., tel. 480/967–8082. AE, D, DC, MC, V. No lunch Mon.–Sat.

Thai

$$ MALEE'S ON MAIN. This fashionable eatery serves up sophisticated, Thai-inspired fare. The recommended ahoi phannee is a medley of seafood in a bamboo-leaf bowl moistened with red curry sauce redolent of coconut, lime leaf, and Thai basil. The Thai barbecued chicken, grilled to a sizzle and coated with rum, is outstanding. Beware: Take Malee's spices seriously—even the "mild" dishes have a bite. 7131 E. Main St., tel. 480/947–6042. AE, DC, MC, V. No lunch Sun.

EAST VALLEY: TEMPE, MESA, CHANDLER

American

$$$–$$$$ **TOP OF THE ROCK.** The iron law of restaurant physics proclaims
★ that food quality declines the higher off the ground you get (airline food is the ultimate proof). But Top of the Rock seems to be the exception to the rule. This beautiful room, set atop a Tempe butte, has panoramic views of the Valley and food that is simply tops. The lobster Napoleon appetizer—lobster layered between crispy wontons lined with Boursin cheese—is good enough to order for entrée and dessert. Main dishes include sugar-spiced barbecue salmon, roasted veal chop, free-range chicken, and mesquite-grilled Black Angus sirloin steak. The house specialty dessert is black bottom pie, with a chocolate praline center and chocolate mousse topping. This is a great spot for a romantic dinner. *2000 Westcourt Way (Buttes Resort), Tempe, tel. 602/225–9000. Reservations essential. AE, D, DC, MC, V. No lunch.*

$$–$$$ **GORDON BIERSCH.** Although it's in the heart of Mill Avenue, right by Arizona State University, Gordon Biersch is hardly your typical college-town watering hole—it's a high-energy brewpub with a range of sophisticated house brews and a menu made for grown-ups. Big picture windows give a great view of Tempe, and the food is just as visually pleasing. Smoked salmon hand-rolls, a skillet of roasted mussels, and beer-batter onion rings are good munchies, and finishing an order of garlic fries requires the help of several friends. The cioppino, oyster pan roast, New York steak, and peppered ahi tuna are winning entrées. And drink up: the brewmaster follows the *Reinheitsgebot*, 500-year-old German guidelines for beer making. It's the reason German beer has the

reputation it does, and the reason why these suds taste so good.
420 S. Mill Ave., Tempe, tel. 480/736–0033. AE, D, DC, MC, V.

Chinese

$$ C-FU GOURMET. This is serious Chinese food, the kind you'd
★ expect to find on Mott Street in New York City's Chinatown or Grant
Street in San Francisco. C-Fu's specialty is fish, and you can see
several species in big holding tanks. If you've ever wondered why
shrimp is a delicacy, it will be clear once you bite into these
crustaceans. After they're fished out of the tank, they're steamed
and bathed in a potent garlic sauce. Clams in black bean sauce
and tilapia in a ginger-scallion sauce also hit all the right buttons.
There's a daily dim sum brunch, too. 2051 W. Warner, Chandler, tel.
480/899–3888. AE, D, DC, MC, V.

Contemporary

$$–$$$ HOUSE OF TRICKS. There's nothing up the sleeves of Robert
and Robin Trick, the inventive chef-proprietors of this rustic-
looking restaurant. The appetizer list is known for its offbeat
creations, such as cheese and avocado blintzes and stuffed grape
leaves in chipotle plum sauce. The main dishes are equally clever.
The roast eggplant and goat cheese lasagna is outstanding.
Grilled rack of pork with a jalapeño-orange marmalade and
scallops in a saffron Pernod sauce also get high marks. The patio
bar is a pleasant place to pass a mild Valley evening. 114 E. 7th St.,
Tempe, tel. 480/968–1114. AE, D, DC, MC, V. Closed Sun.

Ethiopian

$ CAFE LALIBELA. A trip to the Valley's only Ethiopian restaurant
makes for a fun, exotic, and cheap night out. Forget silverware—
Ethiopians scoop up their food with *injera*, a soft, spongy, slightly
sour bread. Among the dishes you can scoop up here are *doro wat*,
chicken and hard-boiled egg in a robust red chile sauce; tikil

gomen, lightly spiced cabbage, carrots, and potatoes; *yebeg tibs*, panfried lamb with green pepper and rosemary; and *fosolia*, spicy green beans cooked with carrot. If you're a vegetarian, Cafe Lalibela becomes even more attractive—try *shiro wat*, ground peas in a red chile sauce, touched up with ginger and garlic. *849 W. University Dr., Tempe, tel. 480/829–1939. AE, D, MC, V. Closed Mon.*

French

$$–$$$ **CITRUS CAFE.** The French proprietors of this café may not boast a fancy Scottsdale address, but they serve some of the best French fare in the Valley. The daily menu is printed on a marker board according to what's fresh in the market. Try the *feuillété aux champignons* (mushrooms in puff pastry) or duck pâté studded with pistachios. The main dishes are pure French comfort food: veal kidneys, sweetbreads, leg of lamb, roast pork, and occasionally even rabbit. For dessert, there's *vacherin*, a marvelous mound of baked meringue that you won't see anyplace else in town. *2330 N. Alma School Rd., Chandler, tel. 480/899–0502. AE, D, DC, MC, V. Closed Sun.–Mon. and Aug. No lunch.*

German

$–$$ **ZUR KATE.** An unpretentious delight with genuine *gemütlichkeit*, this restaurant has a homey congeniality that no interior designer can manufacture. The place is crammed with beer steins, flags, travel posters, and, on weekends, live oom-pah-pah music. The menu covers traditional German territory, which means lots of pork. Some of the favorites are smoked pork chop, ground ham and pork loaf, breaded pork cutlet, and homemade bratwurst. Side dishes are as filling as they are tempting: potato dumplings, home fries, tart potato salad, and pungent sauerkraut. *4815 E. Main St., Mesa, tel. 480/830–4244. Reservations not accepted. MC, V. Closed Sun. (Sun.–Mon. in summer).*

Italian

$ ORGAN STOP PIZZA. If you're towing around kids, this is the place for dinner. The centerpiece of the operation is the mighty Wurlitzer organ, with its 276 keys, 675 stops, and 5,000 pipes. Organists provide continuous entertainment, while the family munches on Italian-American standards—pizza, pasta, sandwiches, and salads. It's all as corny as Kansas in August, and just as wholesome. If you're searching for family values, your search has ended. *1149 E. Southern Ave., Mesa, tel. 480/813–5700. No credit cards.*

Japanese

$$–$$$ YAMAKASA. Yamakasa, one of the Valley's top Japanese restaurants, and its next-door neighbor, C-Fu Gourmet, order their ocean fare in tandem, so you can be sure the high-quality sushi here is fresh. The skilled sushi masters display particular artistry in the hand rolls. Two nabemono (hot pot) dishes are also worth investigating. Another specialty is *shabu-shabu*, thin-sliced beef, swished in a boiling, sake-seasoned, vegetable-filled broth. ("Shabu-shabu" is the hissing sound the meat makes when it hits the liquid.) *2051 W. Warner, Chandler, tel. 480/899–8868. AE, D, DC, MC, V. Closed Mon. No lunch Sun.*

Mediterranean

$–$$ EURO CAFE. If this place had a motto, it would be "Nothing succeeds like excess" when it comes to portion, size, and flavor. The southern Mediterranean-theme fare is staggering, in every sense. The Chicken Palm dish, adorned with palm hearts and artichokes heaped over pasta, could feed a small army. The gyros platter, heaped with capers, sun-dried tomatoes, red peppers, and two kinds of Greek cheeses, is equally generous. And beware the penne carbonara, an unconscionable quantity of pasta tubes fattened with ham and bacon, drenched in a creamy cheese sauce. *1111 S. Longmore, Mesa, tel. 480/962–4224. AE, D, DC, MC, V.*

Mexican

$ ROSA'S MEXICAN GRILL. This festive, family-friendly restaurant summons up images of a Baja beach "taqueria" without the flies. The tacos are Rosa's true glory: beef, pork, and chicken are marinated in fruit juices and herbs for 12 hours, slowly oven-baked for another 10, then shredded and charbroiled. The fish taco, pepped up with cabbage, radishes, and lime, is also in a class by itself. Spoon on one of Rosa's five fresh homemade salsas. But beware the fiery habanero model—it can strip the enamel right off your teeth. *328 E. University Dr., Mesa, tel. 480/964–5451. No credit cards. Closed Sun.–Mon.*

Middle Eastern

$ TASTY KABOB. ★ Persian food is heavily seasoned, but never spicy hot. Perfumed basmati rice, for example, is often teamed with several grilled kabobs—skewers of ground beef, lamb, chicken, or beef tenderloin. The stews here, called *khoresht* and *polo*, also give you a taste of authentic Persian fare. If *baghali polo* is on the menu, don't hesitate—it's dill-infused rice tossed with lima beans and lamb shank. *1250 E. Apache Blvd., Tempe, tel. 480/966–0260. AE, D, MC, V. Closed Mon.*

WEST VALLEY: WEST PHOENIX, GLENDALE, LITCHFIELD PARK

Chinese

$–$$ SILVER DRAGON. ★ This is one of the best Chinese restaurants in town—if you know what you're doing. Non-Asian customers are routinely seated in a small room on the right, and are handed a snoozy, one-from-column-A, one-from-column-B menu. Insist on sitting in the big room to the left, and ask for the Chinese menu (it has brief English descriptions). Your boldness will be rewarded with some of the best Hong Kong–style Chinese fare between the two coasts. "Crispy Hong Kong–Style Chicken" is a dream, a plump whole bird steamed, flash-fried, and hacked into bite-size pieces. The tender, juicy meat and crunchy skin are what yin and yang are all about. Hot-pot dishes, noodles, fish, and vegetarian dishes—the "Buddhist Style Rolls" are riveting—make it hard to eat Chinese food anyplace else in the Valley. 8946 N. 19th Ave., Phoenix, tel. 602/674–0151. AE, MC, V. No lunch Sat.

German

$ HAUS MURPHY'S. Neat, tidy, and friendly, this small German restaurant has as much charm per square foot as any place in town. (The soda fountain came from the set of the movie *Murphy's Romance*.) On weekends, kick back with the old-country accordionist, knock back some old-country brews, and devour the hearty dishes. Schnitzel is a specialty, especially the wonderful paprika version, teamed with crispy chunks of fried potatoes and green beans. Sauerbraten, paired with tart red cabbage and two huge potato dumplings, is not for the faint of appetite. *Kassler kotellett* (smoked pork chops), *rindergulasch* (a lusty beef stew), and a variety of sausage platters will also leave you loosening your belt. The sweet, homey desserts—apple strudel, hazelnut torte—are a nice foil to the smoky, salty fare. 5819 W. Glendale Ave., Glendale, tel. 623/939–2480. AE, D, MC, V.

Mexican

$-$$ PEPE'S TACO VILLA. The neighborhood's not fancy, and neither
★ is this restaurant. But in a town filled with gringoized, south-of-the-border fare, this is the real deal. Tacos rancheros—spicy, shredded pork pungently lathered with adobo paste—are a dream. So are the green corn tamales, *machacado* (air-dried beef), and chiles relleno. But don't leave here without trying the sensational mole, a rich, exotic sauce fashioned from chilies and chocolate. 2108 W. Camelback Rd., Phoenix, tel. 602/242–0379. No credit cards. Closed Tues.

$ LILY'S CAFE. Friendly mom-and-pop proprietors, a jukebox with south-of-the-border hits, and low-priced fresh Mexican fare have kept patrons coming here for almost 50 years. Beef is the featured ingredient. The chimichanga (it's like a deep-fried burrito) is world-class, stuffed with tender beef and covered with cheese, guacamole, and sour cream. Fragrant tamales, spunky red chili beef, and chiles relleno right out of the fryer also shine. *6706 N. 58th Dr., Glendale, tel. 623/937–7757. Reservations not accepted. No credit cards. Closed Mon.–Tues. and Aug.*

Southwestern

$$$–$$$$ ARIZONA KITCHEN. A few years ago, with the help of a researcher who studies Native American foods, management here put together a bold Southwestern menu. Appetizers like blue corn piki rolls, stuffed with capon and goat cheese, and the wild boar Anasazi bean chili give you an indication of what's to come. Entrées include grilled sirloin of buffalo in cabernet-and-vanilla chile negro sauce, and grilled venison medallions in blackberry zinfandel cocoa sauce. For dessert, try the chile-spiked ice cream in the striking turquoise "bowl" of hardened sugar. It's worth the 20-minute drive from downtown Phoenix. *300 E. Indian School Rd. (Wigwam Resort), Litchfield Park, tel. 623/935–3811. AE, D, DC, MC, V. Closed Sun.–Mon. and July–Aug. No lunch.*

Vietnamese

$–$$ LITTLE SAIGON. Less than a decade ago, you could have counted Phoenix's Vietnamese restaurants on one hand, and had enough fingers left over to put in a bowling ball. These days, though, the Vietnamese community is flourishing, and local Vietnamese in-the-know are eating at Little Saigon. The restaurant has a serenity that's out of step with its shopping mall setting—there's a pretty tiled pool with a graceful arched footbridge. The fare is equally serene. Start off with *banh khot*, doughy oval pancakes tinged with coconut and topped with shrimp. Main dishes show a lot of

Eating Well is the Best Revenge

Eating out is a major part of every travel experience. It's a chance to explore flavors you don't find at home. And often the walking you do on vacation means that you can dig in without guilt.

START AT THE TOP By all means take in a really good restaurant or two while you're on the road. A trip is a time to kick back and savor the pleasures of the palate. Read up on the culinary scene before you leave home. Check out representative menus on the Web—some chefs have gone electronic. And ask friends who have just come back. Then reserve a table as far in advance as you can, remembering that the best establishments book up months in advance. Remember that some good restaurants require you to reconfirm the day before or the day of your meal. Then again, some really good places will call you, so make sure to leave a number where you can be reached.

ADVENTURES IN EATING A trip is the perfect opportunity to try food you can't get at home. So leave yourself open to try an ethnic food that's not represented where you live or to eat fruits and vegetables you've never heard of. One of them may become your next favorite food.

BEYOND GUIDEBOOKS You can rely on the restaurants you find in these pages. But also look for restaurants on your own. When you're ready for lunch, ask people you meet where they eat. Look for tiny holes-in-the-wall with a loyal following and the best burgers or crispiest pizza crust. Find out about local chains whose fame rests upon a single memorable dish. There's hardly a food-lover who doesn't relish the chance to share a favorite place. It's fun to come up with your own special find—and asking about food is a great way to start a conversation.

SAMPLE LOCAL FLAVORS Do check out the specialties. Is there a special brand of ice cream or a special dish that you simply must try?

HAVE A PICNIC Every so often eat al fresco. Grocery shopping gives you a whole different view of a place.

spunk, especially the charbroiled beef in grape leaves, lemongrass chicken, and sautéed prawns in a sizzling hot pot. Finish up with Vietnamese coffee, filtered tableside into a cup of sweetened condensed milk. The combustible brew of caffeine, sugar, and fat is one of the best legal jolts anywhere. *1588 W. Montebello Ave. (Christown Mall), Phoenix, tel. 602/864–7582. AE, MC, V.*

$–$$ PHO BANG. Tidy and unpretentious, Pho Bang delivers top-notch Vietnamese fare such as catfish soup, an outstanding broth zipped up with lemon, pineapple, and fennel. Naturally there's *pho*, meal-size noodle soups stocked with various cuts of beef. Splurge on the shrimp and beef specialty and the server returns with three plates: one with transparently thin slices of marinated beef and raw shrimp; one with piles of mint, lettuce, cilantro, pickled leeks, cucumber, and carrot; and one with rice paper. Fire up the portable grill and cook the beef and shrimp. When they're done, combine with the veggies, roll in rice paper, and dip into the national condiment, fish sauce. It's all as good as it sounds. *1702 W. Camelback Rd., Phoenix, tel. 602/433–9440. Reservations not accepted. MC, V.*

In This Chapter

Updated by Cara LaBrie

shopping

SINCE ITS RESORTS BEGAN MULTIPLYING in the 1930s and 1940s, Phoenix has acquired a healthy share of high-style clothiers and leisure-wear boutiques. But long before that, Western clothes dominated fashion here—jeans and boots, cotton shirts and dresses, 10-gallon hats and bola ties (the state's official neckwear). In many places around town, they still do.

On the scene as well, of course, were the arts of the Southwest's true natives—Navajo weavers, sand painters, and silversmiths; Hopi weavers and katsina-doll carvers; Pima and Tohono O'odham (Papago) basket makers and potters; and many more. Inspired by the region's rich cultural traditions, contemporary artists have flourished here, making Phoenix—and in particular Scottsdale, a city with more art galleries than gas stations—one of the Southwest's largest art centers (alongside Santa Fe, New Mexico).

Today's shoppers will find the best of the old and the new—all presented with Southwestern style. Cowboy collectibles, handwoven rugs, traditional Mexican folk art, contemporary turquoise jewelry . . . you'll find them all in the Valley of the Sun. One-of-a-kind shops, upscale stores, and outlet malls offer shoppers everything from cutting-edge, contemporary fashion to more relaxed, down-home styles.

Most of the Valley's power shopping is concentrated in central Phoenix and downtown Scottsdale. But auctions and antiques shops cluster in odd places—and as treasure hunters know, you've always got to keep your eyes open.

Antiques and Collectibles

Downtown **Glendale** along Glendale Avenue and the side streets between 57th and 59th avenues has dozens of antiques stores and a "Gaslight Antique Walk" on the third Thursday evening of each month (every Thursday in December). **Glendale Square Antiques** (7009 N. 58th Ave., tel. 623/435–9952) has a nice collection of glassware, china, and vintage watches. **House of Gera** (7025 N. 58th Ave., tel. 623/842–4631) specializes in Victoriana, particularly jewelry, and houses the offbeat **Rosato Nursing Museum. The Mad Hatter** (5734 W. Glendale Ave., tel. 623/931–1991) is a cavernous space with everything from crystal and Fiestaware to old metal wheels and dusty saddles.

Scottsdale Antique Destination is a group of four stores: **Antique Centre** (2012 N. Scottsdale Rd., tel. 480/675–9500), **Antique Trove** (2020 N. Scottsdale Rd., tel. 480/947–6074), and **Antiques Super-Mall** (1900 N. Scottsdale Rd., tel. 480/874–2900) all have fine antiques and offbeat collectibles, and **Razmataz** (2012 N. Scottsdale Rd., tel. 480/946–9748) offers imported antique and new furniture and decorative items, primarily from Mexico.

Arts and Crafts

The best option, if you're interested in touring Scottsdale's galleries, is the **Art Walk** (tel. 480/990–3939), held from 7 to 9 PM each Thursday year-round (except Thanksgiving). Main Street and Marshall Way, the two major gallery strips, take on a party atmosphere during the evening hours when tourists and locals are browsing.

Art One (4120 N. Marshall Way, Scottsdale, tel. 480/946–5076) features works by local art students; much of what is found here is quite interesting.

Suzanne Brown Galleries (7156 Main St., Scottsdale, tel. 480/945–8475) has a fabulous collection of innovative glasswork, painting, and other fine arts.

Cosanti Originals (6433 Doubletree Ranch Rd., Scottsdale, tel. 480/948–6145) is the studio where architect Paolo Soleri's famous bronze and ceramic wind chimes are made and sold. You can watch the craftspeople hard at work, then pick out your own—prices are surprisingly reasonable.

The **Heard Museum Shop** (22 E. Monte Vista Rd., Phoenix, tel. 602/252–8344) is hands-down the best place in town for Southwestern Native American arts and crafts, both traditional and modern. Prices tend to be high, but quality is assured, with many one-of-a-kind items among their collection of rugs, katsina dolls, pottery, and other crafts; there's also a wide selection of lower-priced gifts. The back room gallery has the latest in native painting and lithographs.

LeKAE Galleries (7175 E. Main St., Scottsdale, tel. 480/874–2624) is a low-pressure, pleasant place to admire some of today's most exciting work. The friendly and discerning staff has scoured the Southwest and beyond for the best in contemporary painting and sculpture.

Mind's Eye (4200 N. Marshall Way, Scottsdale, tel. 480/941–2494) offers an eclectic selection of whimsical art furniture, quilted baskets, bright pottery, and beautifully offbeat kaleidoscopes fashioned from Italian glass, German jewels, and other bits and pieces.

Two Gray Hill (7142 E. 5th Ave., Scottsdale, tel. 480/947–1997 or 888/947–7504) deals in native jewelry, crafts, and katsina dolls. The knowledgeable staff will walk you through the styles and lore of traditional jewelry. They pledge to beat the price of any neighborhood competitor.

Markets

Two of metropolitan Phoenix's best markets can be found in the tiny town of Guadalupe, which is tucked between I–10, Baseline Road, and Warner Road, almost entirely surrounded by the affluent suburb of Tempe. Take I–10 south to Baseline Road, go east ½ mi and turn south on Avenida del Yaqui to find open-air vegetable stalls, roadside fruit stands, and tidy houses covered in flowering vines. **Guadalupe Farmer's Market** (9210 S. Ave. del Yaqui, Guadalupe, tel. 480/730–1945) has all the fresh ingredients you'd find in a rural Mexican market—tomatillos, varieties of chile peppers (fresh and dried), fresh-ground *masa* (cornmeal) for tortillas, cumin and cilantro, and on and on. **Mercado Mexico** (8212 S. Ave. del Yaqui, Guadalupe, tel. 480/831–5925) carries ceramic, paper, tin, and lacquerware, all at unbeatable prices.

In Phoenix, **Patriot's Square Marketplace** (Patriot's Square Park, Washington St. and Central Ave., tel. 623/848–1234) sells arts and crafts, locally grown produce, baked goods, and homemade jams and salsas, livening up downtown every Wednesday from 10 AM to 2 PM, October through April.

Shopping Centers

Arizona Mills (5000 Arizona Mills Circle, Tempe, tel. 480/491–9700), the latest entry in the discount shopping sweepstakes, is a mammoth center featuring almost 200 outlet stores, a food court, cinemas, and faux rain forest.

Biltmore Fashion Park (24th St. and Camelback Rd., Phoenix, tel. 602/955–8400) has posh shops lining its open-air walkways, as well as some of the city's most popular restaurants and cafés. **Macy's** and **Saks Fifth Avenue** are its anchors, and high-end designer boutiques are its stock-in-trade—**Via Veneto, Gucci,** and **Polo by Ralph Lauren** are among them. **Cornelia Park** offers an awe-inspiring collection of MacKenzie-Childs, Ltd., glassware as well as furnishings, tiles, and linens. Home to RoxSand, Sam's Cafe, and Christopher & Paola's Fermier Brasserie, this center has more fine eating in a small radius than anywhere else in Arizona.

The Borgata (6166 N. Scottsdale Rd., tel. 480/998–1822), a re-creation of the Italian village of San Gimignano, is one of the Valley's most fashionable places to shop and home to some of

Scottsdale's most popular restaurants. Shops include **Capriccio** for women's wear, **Stefan Mann** for leather goods, **DaVinci** for menswear, and scores of others. Check out the affordable and intriguing **Mineral & Fossil Gallery** near the Coffee Plantation.

Two-tiered **El Pedregal Festival Marketplace** (Scottsdale Rd. and Carefree Hwy., tel. 480/488–1072), 30 minutes north of downtown Scottsdale, is an attractive shopping plaza. At the foot of a 250-ft boulder formation, it contains posh boutiques and the **Heard Museum North** (tel. 480/488–9817), a satellite of the downtown Heard with its own gift shop. Visit **Casualis** for men's sportswear, **Carefree Casuals** for wearable art for women, **Conrad** for custom leather goods, and **Canyon Lifestyles** for Southwestern furniture and decor items. In the spring and summer there are open-air Thursday-night concerts in the courtyard amphitheater.

Metrocenter (I–17 and Peoria Ave., tel. 602/997–2641), on the west side of Phoenix, is the kind of enclosed double-deck, Muzak-choked sterile environment that made mall a four-letter word. Anchor department stores are **Dillard's, JCPenney, Macy's, Robinsons-May,** and **Sears.** Adjacent to the mall, a roller coaster zips through Taj Mahal–esque minarets at **Castles 'N' Coasters** (9445 N. Metro Pkwy. E, tel. 602/997–7575), where a miniature golf park and video-game palace round out the fun.

Mill Avenue in Tempe is the main drag for ASU's student population; small, interesting shops and eateries make for great browsing or just hanging out. **Urban Outfitters** (545 S. Mill Ave., tel. 480/966–7250) sells rough-edged, trendy gear and affordable housewares. The very cool **Changing Hands Bookstore** (414 Mill Ave., tel. 480/966–0203) has three stories of new and used books and an inviting atmosphere that will tempt you to linger—as many students do.

Paradise Valley Mall (Cactus Rd. and Tatum Blvd., tel. 480/996–8840), in northeastern Phoenix, is an older mall with a Macy's department store.

Beyond T-Shirts and Key Chains

You can't go wrong with baseball caps, refrigerator magnets, beer mugs, sweatshirts, T-shirts, key chains, and other local logo merchandise. You won't go broke buying these items, either.

BUDGET FOR A MAJOR PURCHASE If souvenirs are all about keeping the memories alive in the long haul, plan ahead to shop for something really special—a work of art, a rug or something else hand-crafted, or a major accessory for your home. One major purchase will stay with you far longer than a dozen tourist trinkets, and you'll have all the wonderful memories associated with shopping for it besides.

ADD TO YOUR COLLECTION Whether antiques, used books, salt and pepper shakers, or ceramic frogs are your thing, start looking in the first day or two. Chances are you'll want to scout around and then go back to some of the first shops you visited before you hand over your credit card.

GET GUARANTEES IN WRITING Is the vendor making promises? Ask him to put them in writing.

ANTICIPATE A SHOPPING SPREE If you think you might buy breakables, include a length of bubble wrap. Pack a large tote bag in your suitcase in case you need extra space. Don't fill your suitcase to bursting before you leave home. Or include some old clothing that you can leave behind to make room for new acquisitions.

KNOW BEFORE YOU GO Study prices at home on items you might consider buying while you're away. Otherwise you won't recognize a bargain when you see one.

PLASTIC, PLEASE Especially if your purchase is pricey and you're looking for authenticity, it's always smart to pay with a credit card. If a problem arises later on and the merchant can't or won't resolve it, the credit-card company may help you out.

At boisterous **Scottsdale Fashion Square** (Scottsdale and Camelback Rds., Scottsdale, tel. 480/941–2140), retractable skylights open to reveal sunny skies above. Besides Robinsons-May and Dillard's, there is **Neiman Marcus** (check out the hanging Paolo Soleri sculpture above the Neiman's elevator). The collection of stores runs toward the pricey chains including **J. Crew** and **Artafax. FAO Schwarz,** the **Disney Store,** and **Warner Bros. Studio Store** are attractions for kids.

Superstition Springs Center (AZ 60 and Superstition Springs Rd., Mesa, tel. 480/832–0212), 30 mi east of Phoenix, has the usual complement of shops and eateries, plus a pleasant outdoor cactus garden to stroll in. The handsome indoor carousel and 15-ft Gila-monster slide keep the kids occupied.

In This Chapter

Updated by Cara LaBrie

outdoor activities and sports

CENTRAL ARIZONA HAS AMPLE OPPORTUNITY for outdoor recreation, but the area's dry desert heat imposes particular restraints—even in winter, hikers and cyclists should wear lightweight opaque clothing, a hat or visor, and high UV-rated sunglasses and should carry a quart of water for each hour of activity. The intensity of the sun makes strong sunscreen (SPF 15 or higher) a must, and don't forget to apply it to your hands and feet. From May 1 to October 1, you shouldn't jog or hike from one hour after sunrise until a half hour before sunset. During those times, the air is so hot and dry that your body will lose moisture at a dangerous, potentially lethal rate. Don't head out to desert areas at night, however, to jog or hike in the summer; that's when rattlesnakes and scorpions are on the prowl.

PARTICIPANT SPORTS
Bicycling

Although the terrain is relatively level, the desert climate can be tough on cyclists; note the advice on hours and clothing, *above*. Be sure to have a helmet and a mirror when riding in the streets: there are few adequate bike lanes in the Valley.

Scottsdale's Indian Bend Wash (along Hayden Road, from Shea Boulevard south to Indian School Road) has bikeable paths winding among its golf courses and ponds. **Pinnacle Peak,** about 25 mi northeast of downtown Phoenix, is a popular place to take bikes for the ride north to Carefree and Cave Creek, or east and south over the mountain pass and down to the Verde River, toward Fountain Hills. Mountain bikers will want to check out the **Trail 100,** which runs throughout the Phoenix Mountain preserve (enter at Dreamy Draw park, just east of the intersection of Northern Avenue and 16th Street). **Cave Creek** and **Carefree,** in the foothills about 30 mi northeast of Phoenix, offer pleasant riding with a wide range of stopover options. **South Mountain Park** (☞ Hiking, *below*) is the prime site for mountain bikers, with its 40-plus mi of trails—some of them with challenging ascents and all of them quiet and scenic.

For rentals, contact **Wheels N' Gear** (7607 E. McDowell Rd., Scottsdale, tel. 480/945–2881). For detailed maps of bike paths, contact **Phoenix Parks and Recreation** (tel. 602/262–6861). To get in touch with fellow bike enthusiasts and find out about regular and special-event rides, contact the **The Arizona Bicycle Club, Inc** (Gene or Sylvia Berlatsky, tel. 602/264–5478), the state's largest group. Popular Sunday-morning rides start in Phoenix's **Granada Park** (20th St. and Maryland Ave.) and end up at a local breakfast spot. **Desert Biking Adventures** (tel. 602/320–4602 or 888/249–2453) offers two-, three-, and four-hour mountain-biking excursions through the Sonoran Desert.

Four-Wheeling

Taking a jeep or a wide-track Humvee through the backcountry has become a popular way to experience the desert terrain's saguaro-covered mountains and curious rock formations. A number of companies offer four-wheeling packages for $50–$75 for short excursions.

Arizona Awareness Desert Jeep Tours (tel. 480/860–1777) ventures down to the Verde River on its own trail and offers wilderness cookouts.

Arrowhead Desert Jeep Tours (tel. 602/942–3361 or 800/514–9063), run by a self-described "hard-core prospector who fell in love with tourism," offers adventures that include gold panning on a private claim, cookouts, cattle drives, river crossings, and Native American dance demonstrations.

Rawhide Land and Cattle Company (tel. 480/488–0023 or 800/294–5337) travels into the Tonto National Forest on rugged old stage and mining roads, stopping for botany lessons, explorations of Hohokam ruins and a gold mine, and a six-gun target shoot along the way.

Scottsdale Jeep Rentals (tel. 480/951–2191) rents jeeps and provides free trail maps to those who prefer to drive themselves and forgo the company of a talkative guide.

Golf

Arizona boasts more golf courses per capita than any other state west of the Mississippi River, an embarrassment of riches that, coupled with its surfeit of sunny days, makes the Grand Canyon State a golfer's paradise. The world-class courses are among Arizona's major industries, with new spots popping up seemingly on a daily basis: more than 100 courses are available (some lighted at night), and the PGA's Southwest section has its headquarters here. For a detailed listing, contact the **Arizona Golf Association** (7226 N. 16th St., Phoenix 85020, tel. 602/944–3035 or 800/458–8484).

Ahwatukee Country Club (12432 S. 48th St., tel. 480/893–9772), an upscale course just south of South Mountain Park, is semiprivate but also has a public driving range.

Arizona Biltmore (24th St. and Missouri Ave., tel. 602/955–9655), the granddaddy of Phoenix golf courses, offers two 18-hole PGA championship courses, lessons, and clinics.

One of the latest entries into the Valley's golf scene, **Chiricahua at Desert Mountain** (10333 Rockaway Hills, Scottsdale, tel. 480/488–1362) is a player-friendly course designed by Jack Nicklaus.

Encanto Park (2775 N. 15th Ave., Phoenix, tel. 602/253–3963) is an attractive, affordable public course.

Gold Canyon Golf Club (6100 S. Kings Ranch Rd., Gold Canyon, tel. 480/982–9090) is a desert course backed by the stunning Superstition Mountains.

The championship **Grayhawk Golf Club** (8620 E. Thompson Peak Pkwy., Scottsdale, tel. 480/502–1800) is pricey, but it's rated one of the top public courses in Arizona. Designed by Tom Fazio, the course is immaculately groomed.

Hillcrest Golf Club (20002 N. Star Ridge, Sun City West, tel. 623/584–1500) is the best course in the Sun Cities, with 179 acres of well-designed turf.

Papago Golf Course (5595 E. Moreland St., tel. 602/275–8428) is a low-price public course in a scenic city setting and Phoenix's best municipal course.

Raven Golf Club at South Mountain (3636 E. Baseline Rd., Phoenix, tel. 602/243–3636) has thousands of drought-resistant Aleppo pines and Lombardy poplars, making it a cool, shady haven for summertime golfers.

Sun Ridge Canyon (13100 N. Sun Ridge Dr., Fountain Hills, tel. 480/837–5100) is an 18-hole championship course with an inspiring view of the canyon scenery.

Thunderbird Country Club (701 E. Thunderbird Trail, Phoenix, tel. 602/243–1262) has 18 holes of championship-rated play on the north slopes of South Mountain. Sweeping views of the city are a bonus.

Tournament Players Club of Scottsdale (17020 N. Hayden Rd., Scottsdale, tel. 480/585–3600), a 36-hole course by Tom Weiskopf and Jay Morrish, is the site of the PGA Phoenix Open.

Troon North (10320 E. Dynamite Blvd., Scottsdale, tel. 480/585–5300) offers a challenging 36-hole course, designed by Weiskopf and Morrish, that makes excellent use of the desert landscape.

Health Clubs

The **Arizona Athletic Club** (1425 W. 14th St., Tempe, tel. 480/
894–2281), near the airport at the border between Tempe and
Scottsdale, is the Valley's largest facility. Nonmembers pay a day
rate of $12, but the club has arrangements with some area
hotels.

Jazzercise (tel. 800/348–4748) has 13 franchised sites in the
Valley.

Naturally Women (2827 W. Peoria Ave., Phoenix, tel. 602/678–
4000; 3320 S. Price Rd., Tempe, tel. 602/838–8800), closed
Sunday, focuses on women's needs, from health profiles to diet
and exercise programs; it offers one free visit, and a daily rate of
$10 thereafter.

The **YMCA** (tel. 602/528–5540) offers full facilities—including
weight rooms, aerobics classes, pool, and racquetball
privileges—to nonmembers at several Valley locations. Pool
rates are $8 per day.

Hiking

The Valley has some of the best desert mountain hiking in the
world—the **Phoenix Mountain Preserve System** (tel. 602/262–
6861), in the mountains that surround the city, has its own park
rangers who can help plan your hikes. Phoenix's hiking trails are
some of the most heavily used in the world—and for good reason.

Camelback Mountain (North of Camelback Rd. on 48th St., tel.
602/256–3220), another landmark hike, has no park, and the
trails are more difficult. This is for intermediate to experienced
hikers.

The **Papago Peaks** (Van Buren St. and Galvin Pkwy., tel. 602/
256–3220) were sacred sites for the Tohono O'odham tribe and
probably the Hohokam before them. The soft sandstone peaks
contain accessible caves, some petroglyphs, and splendid views
of much of the Valley. This is another good spot for family hikes.

South Mountain Park (10919 S. Central Ave., tel. 602/261–8457) is the jewel of the city's Mountain Park Preserves. Its mountains and arroyos contain more than 40 mi of marked and maintained trails—all open to hikers, horseback riders, and mountain bikers. It also has three auto-accessible lookout points, with 65-mi sight lines. Rangers can help you plan hikes to view some of the 200 petroglyph sites.

Squaw Peak Summit Trail (2701 E. Squaw Peak Dr., just north of Lincoln Dr., tel. 602/262–7901) ascends the landmark mountain at a steep 19% grade, but children can handle the 1¼-mi hike if adults take it slowly—allow about 1½ hours for each direction. Call ahead to schedule an easy hike with a ranger, who will introduce desert geology, flora, and fauna.

Horseback Riding

More than two dozen stables and equestrian tour outfitters in the Valley attest to the saddle's enduring importance in Arizona—even in this auto-dominated metropolis.

All Western Stables (10220 S. Central Ave., Phoenix, tel. 602/276–5862), one of several stables at the entrance to South Mountain Park, offers rentals, guided rides, hayrides, and cookouts.

MacDonald's Ranch (26540 N. Scottsdale Rd., Scottsdale, tel. 480/585–0239) offers one- and two-hour trail rides and guided breakfast, lunch, and dinner rides through desert foothills above Scottsdale.

Superstition Stables (Windsong and Meridian Rds., Apache Junction, tel. 480/982–5488) is licensed to lead tours throughout the entire Superstition Mountains area for more experienced riders; easier rides are also available.

Hot-Air Ballooning

A sunrise or sunset hot-air-balloon ascent is a remarkable desert sightseeing experience. The average fee—there are more than three dozen companies to chose from—is $135 per person, and hotel pickup is usually included. Since flight paths and landing sites vary with wind speeds and directions, a roving land crew follows each balloon in flight. Time in the air is generally between 1 and 1½ hours, but allow three hours for the total excursion. Be prepared for changing temperatures as the sun rises or sets, but it's not actually any colder up in the balloon.

Adventures Out West (tel. 602/996–6100 or 800/755–0935) will send you home with a free video of your flight taped from the balloon.

Hot Air Expeditions (tel. 480/502–6999 or 800/831–7610) offers the best ballooning in Phoenix. Flights are long, the staff is charming, and the gourmet treats are out of this world.

Unicorn Balloon Company (tel. 480/991–3666 or 800/468–2478), operating since 1978, is run by the state's ballooning examiner for the FAA. Located at Scottsdale Airport, it offers free pickup at many area hotels.

Jogging

Phoenix's unique 200-mi network of canals provides a naturally cooled (and often landscaped) scenic track throughout the metro area. Two other popular jogging areas are Phoenix's **Encanto Park,** 3 mi northwest of Civic Plaza, and Scottsdale's **Indian Bend Wash,** which runs for more than 5 mi along Hayden Road. Both have lagoons and tree-shaded greens.

Sailplaning

At the Estrella Sailport, **Arizona Soaring Inc.** (tel. 480/821–2903 or 800/861–2318) gives sailplane rides in a basic trainer or high-performance plane for prices ranging from $69 to $89. The adventuresome can opt for a wild 15-minute acrobatic flight for $99.

Tennis

Hole-in-the-Wall Racquet Club (7677 N. 16th St., tel. 602/997–2626), at the Pointe Hilton at Squaw Peak (☞ Where to Stay), has eight paved courts available for same-day reservation at $18 per half hour.

Kiwanis Park Recreation Center (6111 S. All America Way, Tempe, tel. 480/350–5201, ext. 4) has 15 lighted premier-surface courts (all for same-day or one-day-advance reserve). Before 5 PM, courts rent for $4.50, after 5 PM, the rate is $6; $2 drop-in programs are offered for single players weekdays, 10:30–noon.

Mountain View Tennis Center (1104 E. Grovers Ave., tel. 602/788–6088), just north of Bell Road, is a Phoenix city facility with 20 lighted courts that can be reserved for $3 for 90 minutes of singles play during the day; after dark, the light fee is $2.20.

Phoenix Civic Plaza Sports Complex (121 E. Adams St., tel. 602/256–4120) has three lighted rooftop courts available for $4–$6.

Phoenix Tennis Center (6330 N. 21st Ave., tel. 602/249–3712), a city facility with 22 lighted hard courts, charges $1.50 per person for 1½ hours on the courts; if it's after dark, add a $2.20 light fee.

Watering Hole Racquet Club (901-C E. Saguaro Dr., tel. 602/997–7237) has nine hard, lighted courts that rent for $15 per hour.

Tubing

In a region not known for water, one indigenous aquatic sport has developed: Tubing—riding an inner tube down calm water and mild rapids—has become a very popular tradition on the Salt and Verde rivers. Outfitters that rent tubes include **Salt River Recreation** (Usery Pass and Power Rds., Mesa, tel. 480/984–3305), conveniently located and offering shuttle-bus service to and from your starting point. Tubes are $9 per day, all day 9–4; tubing season runs May–September.

SPECTATOR SPORTS
Auto Racing

Phoenix International Raceway (11901 W. Baseline Rd., Avondale, tel. 602/252–3833), the Valley's NASCAR track, hosts the Skoal Bandit Copper World Classic, Phoenix 200 Indy Car race, and Phoenix 500 NASCAR race.

Balloon Racing

The **Thunderbird Hot-Air-Balloon Classic** (tel. 602/978–7208) has grown into two days of festivities surrounding the national invitational balloon race, held the first weekend in November. You haven't lived till you've seen the Valley skies filled with brightly colored balloons.

Baseball

Many professional baseball teams conduct spring training in Arizona. Games start at the end of February; **Dillard's** (tel. 480/503–5555) sells tickets. To obtain more information about spring training in Arizona, contact the following Cactus League teams:

Anaheim Angels, Tempe Diablo Stadium, Tempe, tel. 602/784–4444.

Arizona Diamondbacks, Tucson Electric Park, Tucson, tel. 888/777–4664.

Chicago Cubs, HoHoKam Park, Mesa, tel. 602/503–5555.

Chicago White Sox, Tucson Electric Park, Tucson, tel. 800/638–4253.

Colorado Rockies, Hi Corbett Field, Tucson, tel. 520/327–9467.

Milwaukee Brewers, Maryvale Baseball Park, Phoenix, tel. 602/895–1200.

Oakland A's, Phoenix Municipal Stadium, Peoria, tel. 602/392–0217.

San Francisco Giants, Scottsdale Stadium, Scottsdale, tel. 602/990–7972.

Seattle Mariners, Peoria Stadium, Peoria, tel. 602/412–9000.

The **Arizona Diamondbacks** (tel. 602/514–8400), Phoenix's Major League team, plays at the Bank One Ballpark (☞ Downtown Phoenix in Here and There). The 48,500-seat stadium has a retractable roof, a natural-grass playing surface, and a slew of restaurants, luxury boxes, and party suites.

Basketball

The **Phoenix Suns** (tel. 602/379–7867) continues to fill all 19,000 spectator seats in the America West Arena (☞ Downtown Phoenix in Here and There); Valley basketball fans are fiercely loyal to the team. Tip-off is usually at 7 PM.

Football

The **Arizona Cardinals** (tel. 602/379–0102), the area's professional football team, plays at ASU's Sun Devil Stadium in Tempe.

On New Year's Eve at Sun Devil Stadium is the **Fiesta Bowl** (tel. 480/350–0911), one of college football's most important bowl games.

Golf

The **Phoenix Open** (tel. 602/870–0163), in January at the Tournament Players Club of Scottsdale, is a major PGA Tour event and draws an estimated 400,000 spectators each year. In March, women compete in the **Standard Register PING Tournament** (tel. 602/942–0000), at the Moon Valley Country Club.

Hockey

The **Phoenix Coyotes** (tel. 602/379–7825) faces off in the America West Arena (☞ Downtown Phoenix in Here and There);

whether you come for the checking and hooking or to watch the Zamboni, take a moment to enjoy the small irony of artificial ice in the desert.

Rodeos

The **Parada del Sol,** held each January by the Scottsdale Jaycees (tel. 480/990–3179), includes a rodeo, a lavish parade famed for its silver-studded saddles, and a 200-mi daredevil ride from Holbrook down the Mogollon Rim to Scottsdale by the Hashknife Pony Express. The **Rodeo of Rodeos,** sponsored in March by the Phoenix Jaycees (4133 N. 7th St., tel. 602/263–8671), opens with one of the Southwest's oldest and best parades.

In This Chapter

Updated by Cara LaBrie

nightlife and the arts

FROM BREWPUBS, SPORTS BARS, AND coffeehouses, to dance clubs, mega-concerts, and country venues, the Valley of the Sun offers nightlife of all types. Nightclubs, comedy clubs, and upscale lounges—whatever your choice for fun, nightlife abounds in downtown Phoenix, along Camelback Road in north-central Phoenix, and in Scottsdale, Tempe, and other suburbs.

Among music and dancing styles, country-and-western has the longest tradition here; jazz, surprisingly, runs a close second. Rock clubs and hotel lounges are also numerous and varied. The Valley attracts a steady stream of pop and rock acts. Phoenix is getting hipper and more cosmopolitan as it gets older: cigar-lovers and martini-sippers will find a wealth of opportunities to indulge their tastes. There are also more than 30 gay and lesbian bars, centered primarily on 7th Avenue, 7th Street, and the stretch of Camelback Road between the two.

You can find listings and reviews in the *New Times* (www.phoenixnewtimes.com) free weekly newspaper, distributed Wednesday, and *The Rep Entertainment Guide* of the *Arizona Republic*. PHX Downtown, a free monthly available in downtown establishments, has an extensive calendar for the neighborhood's events from art exhibits and poetry readings to professional sporting events. For concert tickets, try **Dillard's ticket line** (tel. 480/503–5555 or 800/638–4253).

Phoenix's performing-arts groups have grown rapidly in number and sophistication, especially during the past two decades. The permanent home of the Arizona Theatre Company, Actors Theatre of Phoenix, and Ballet Arizona, the **Herberger Theater Center** (200 W. Washington St., tel. 602/534–5600) also presents a variety of visiting dance troupes and orchestras.

The **Orpheum Theatre** (203 W. Adams St., tel. 602/252–9678; ☞ Downtown Phoenix in Here and There) showcases various performing arts, including children's theater, and film festivals. Facing the Herberger Theater, **Symphony Hall** (225 E. Adams St., tel. 602/262–7272) is home to the Phoenix Symphony and Arizona Opera as well as a venue for pop concerts by top-name performers. Arizona State University offers a variety of events ranging from touring Broadway shows to jazz, pop, and classical concerts at three fine venues: the **Gammage Auditorium** (Mill Ave. at Apache Blvd., Tempe, tel. 480/965–3434), **Kerr Cultural Center** (6110 N. Scottsdale Rd., Scottsdale, tel. 480/965–5377), and the **Sundome Center** (19403 R. H. Johnson Blvd., Sun City West, tel. 623/975–1900).

The most comprehensive ticket agencies for ASU events are the **Arizona State University Public Events Box Office** (Gammage Center, Tempe, tel. 480/965–3434) and **Dillard's ticket line** (tel. 480/503–5555 or 800/638–4253).

For weekly listings of theater, arts, and music events, check out *The Rep Entertainment Guide,* in Thursday's *Arizona Republic,* or pick up an issue of the independent weekly, *New Times,* from street corner boxes.

NIGHTLIFE
Bars and Lounges

America's Original Sports Bar (455 N. 3rd St., Arizona Center, tel. 602/252–2112) offers more than 40,000 square ft of boisterous fun, with 62 TVs (seven giant screens among them).

AZ88 (7353 Scottsdale Mall, Scottsdale, tel. 480/994–5576) has the vibe of a big-city bar and an artful interior. Casual dining and comfortable surroundings make this a perennial favorite of all ages.

Beeloe's Cafe and Underground Bar (501 S. Mill Ave., Tempe, tel. 480/894–1230) is everything you'd expect in this hip college town, with eclectic presentations of visual and musical artists. As the name implies, the bar is located in the basement.

Cajun House (7117 E. 3rd Ave., Scottsdale, tel. 480/945–5150), currently one of the hottest spots in the area, is the Valley's only Louisiana-themed venue. Join locals who sip Hurricanes while listening to rock, jazz, and Cajun music; on weekends there's a line to get in.

The Famous Door (7419 Indian Plaza, Scottsdale, tel. 480/970–1945) specializes in martinis and cigars. Relax to the sounds of local jazz artists on weekends.

Liquori's (2309 E. Indian School Rd., Phoenix, tel. 602/957–2444) features one of the longest happy hours in Phoenix (10 AM–8 PM). As you shoot pool or play pinball, the jukebox turns out hard rock, alternative rock, and blues.

Majerle's Sports Grill (24 N. 2nd St., tel. 602/253–9004), operated by former Suns basketball player Dan Majerle, is within striking distance of the major sports facilities and offers a comprehensive menu as well as a bar for postgame celebrations (or sorrow-drowning).

Top of the Rock Bar (2000 W. Westcourt Way, Tempe, tel. 602/431–2370), the lounge in Top of the Rock restaurant (☞ Eating Out) at the Buttes, attracts an older, professional crowd to drink in cocktails and the city's most spectacular view.

Casinos

Just northeast of Scottsdale, **Fort McDowell Casino** (2 mi east of Shea Blvd. on AZ 87, tel. 602/843–3678 or 800/843–3678) is popular with the Scottsdale-resort crowd. In addition to the cards, slots, and keno games, off-track greyhound wagering takes place in a classy, mahogany room with 18 giant video screens. Take advantage of the casino's Valley-wide shuttle.

Clubs

Axis and Radius (7340 E. Indian Plaza Rd., Scottsdale, tel. 480/970–1112) is the dress-to-kill locale where you can party and hobnob with celebrities. Michael Jordan, George Clooney, and Cher are just some of the beautiful people who've rocked at these side-by-side clubs. Axis features high-energy dance music and Top 40 hits, whereas Radius pumps up the high-energy funk.

Bobby McGee's (7000 E. Shea Blvd., Scottsdale, tel. 480/998–5591) is one of the Valley's most popular spots for DJ-spun music.

Downside Risk (7419 E. Indian Plaza Rd., Scottsdale, tel. 480/945–3304) is a sure bet for a happening young crowd in the mood to libate and gyrate.

Martini Ranch & MR Sports Bar (7295 E. Stetson Dr., Scottsdale, tel. 480/970–0500) attracts singles to its patio where alternative and classic rock bands play Tuesday through Saturday.

Tapas Papa Frita (6826 E. 5th Ave., Scottsdale, tel. 480/424–7777) really turns up the heat. Fiery salsa rhythms will have you up and dancing the merengue, the cha-cha, and the mambo.

Coffeehouses

Willow House (149 W. McDowell Rd., Phoenix, tel. 602/252–0272) is a self-described artist's cove that draws scores of artsy, bohemian-types—a uniquely fun and funky spot in a city not overflowing with great coffeehouses. Thursday-night poetry readings are a big draw. The espresso flows until midnight on weeknights, 1 AM on weekends.

Comedy

The Improv (930 E. University Dr., Tempe, tel. 480/921–9877), part of a national chain, showcases better-known headliners Thursday–Sunday; shows cost between $10 and $20.

Star Theater (7117 E. McDowell Rd., Scottsdale, tel. 480/423–0120) features comedy for people of all ages, including kids, performed by Oxymoron'Z Improvisational Troupe on Friday and Saturday nights and stand-up comics the last two Thursdays of each month; reservations are required.

Country and Western

Handlebar-J (7116 E. Becker La., Scottsdale, tel. 480/948–0110) has a lively, 10-gallon-hat–wearing crowd.

At **Mr. Lucky's** (3660 N.W. Grand Ave., tel. 602/246–0686), the granddaddy of Phoenix Western clubs, you can dance the two-step all night (or learn how, if you haven't before).

The **Red River Music Hall** (730 N. Mill Ave., Tempe, tel. 480/829–6779) is a lively venue that hosts all kinds of concerts, including a jazz series, country music concerts, and special Christmas shows.

The **Rockin' Horse Saloon** (7316 E. Stetson Dr., Scottsdale, tel. 480/949–0992) features baby back ribs, live Western music, and dancing in a setting guaranteed to bring out the cowboy or cowgirl in you.

Gay and Lesbian Bars

Ain't Nobody's Business (3031 E. Indian School Rd., Phoenix, tel. 602/224–9977) is the most popular lesbian bar in town; you'll also find a few gay men at this male-friendly establishment, well-known as one of the most fun in town.

B.S. West (7125 E. 5th Ave., Scottsdale, tel. 480/945–9028) draws a stylish, well-heeled crowd to this location tucked in a shopping center on Scottsdale's main shopping drag.

Charlie's (727 W. Camelback Rd., Phoenix, tel. 602/265–0224), a longtime favorite of local gay men, has a country-western look (cowboy hats are the accessory of choice) and friendly staff.

Young men go to the **Crowbar** (710 N. Central Ave., Phoenix, tel. 602/258–8343) to see and be seen; it's where Phoenix's beautiful people hang out.

Jazz

For a current schedule of jazz happenings, call the **Jazz in AZ Hotline** (tel. 602/254–4545).

J. Chew & Co. (7320 Scottsdale Mall, Scottsdale, tel. 480/946–2733) is a cozy, popular spot with indoor and outdoor seating. It's the place to find up-and-coming jazz performers while enjoying a tasty hot or cold sandwich.

Orbit Cafe (40 E. Camelback Rd., Phoenix, tel. 602/265–2354) has live jazz and blues every evening in a contemporary art deco–style setting with a casual ambience.

Timothy's (6335 N. 16th St., Phoenix, tel. 602/277–7634) brings together fine French-influenced Southwestern cuisine with top jazz performances from 8:30 to 12:30 nightly, and there's no cover charge.

Microbreweries

Bandersnatch Brew Pub (125 E. 5th St., Tempe, tel. 480/966–4438) is a popular, unhurried student hangout that brews several *cervezas* daily.

Coyote Springs Brewing Co. (4883 N. 20th St., at Camelback Rd., Phoenix, tel. 602/468–0403; 122 E. Washington St., Phoenix, tel. 602/256–6645), the oldest brewpub in Phoenix, has delicious handcrafted ales and lagers, and a thriving patio scene at the 20th Street location. Try a raspberry brew.

Hops! Bistro & Brewery (7000 E. Camelback Rd., Scottsdale Fashion Square, tel. 480/946–1272; 8668 E. Shea Blvd., Scottsdale, tel. 480/998–7777) serves up bistro cuisine and fills chilled mugs with amber and wheat drafts from the display brewery.

Rock and Blues

The **Blue Note** (8040 E. McDowell Rd., Scottsdale, tel. 480/946–6227) is a blues club with live shows every night. Friday and Saturday there's a $5 cover.

Char's Has the Blues (4631 N. 7th Ave., tel. 602/230–0205) is the top Valley blues club with nightly bands.

Long Wong's on Mill (701 S. Mill Ave., Tempe, tel. 480/966–3147) may not be the most elegant joint you'll ever see, but huge crowds of students and other grungy types pack the crowded, graffiti-covered room to catch the sounds of local musicians playing acoustic, rockabilly, rock, and blues.

Mason Jar (2303 E. Indian School Rd., Phoenix, tel. 602/956–6271) has nightly shows, mostly hard rock.

Rhythm Room (1019 E. Indian School Rd., Phoenix, tel. 602/265–4842) hosts a variety of local and touring blues artists.

THE ARTS
Classical Music

Arizona Opera (4600 N. 12th St., Phoenix, tel. 602/266–7464), one of the nation's most respected regional companies, stages an opera season, primarily classical, in Tucson and Phoenix. The Phoenix season runs October to March at Symphony Hall (☞ *above*).

Phoenix Symphony Orchestra (455 N. 3rd St., Suite 390, Phoenix, tel. 602/495–1999), the resident company at Symphony Hall (☞ *above*), has reached the top rank of American regional symphonies. Its season includes orchestral works from classical and contemporary literature, a chamber series, composer festivals, and outdoor pops concerts.

Dance

A. Ludwig Co. (tel. 480/966–3391), the Valley's foremost modern dance troupe, includes choreography by founder-director Ann Ludwig, an ASU faculty member, in its repertoire of contemporary works.

Ballet Arizona (3645 E. Indian School Rd., tel. 602/381–1096), the state's professional ballet company, presents a full season of classical and contemporary works (including pieces commissioned for the company) in Tucson and in Phoenix, where it performs at the Herberger Theater Center, Symphony Hall, and Gammage Auditorium (☞ *above*).

Film

If you're looking for something besides the latest blockbuster, the **Valley Art Theatre** (509 S. Mill Ave., Tempe, tel. 480/829–6668) shows major foreign releases and domestic art films.

Galleries

The gallery scene in Phoenix and Scottsdale is so extensive that your best bet is to consult the "art exhibits" listings in the weekly *New Times* or Thursday's *The Rep Entertainment Guide* put out by the *Arizona Republic*. Or simply stroll down to Main Street and Marshall Way in downtown Scottsdale to view the best art the Valley has to offer.

Theater and Shows

Actors Theatre of Phoenix (tel. 602/253–6701) is the resident theater troupe at the Herberger (☞ *above*). The theater presents a full season of drama, comedy, and musical productions.

Arizona Theatre Company (502 W. Roosevelt, tel. 602/256–6995 or 602/252–8497) is the only resident company in the country with a two-city (Tucson and Phoenix) operation. Productions range from classic dramas to musicals and new works by emerging playwrights.

Black Theater Troupe (333 E. Portland St., tel. 602/258–8128) performs at its own house, the Helen K. Mason Center, a half block from the city's Performing Arts Building on Deck Park. It presents original and contemporary dramas and musical revues, as well as adventurous adaptations.

Childsplay (tel. 480/350–8112) is the state's professional theater company for young audiences and families. Rotating through many a venue—Herberger Theater Center, Scottsdale Center for the Arts, and Tempe Performing Arts Center—these players deliver colorful, high-energy performances of works ranging from adaptations of *Charlotte's Web* and *The Velveteen Rabbit* to a theatrical salute to surrealist painter René Magritte and the power of imagination.

Great Arizona Puppet Theatre (302 W. Latham St., tel. 602/262–2050), happily relocated to a historic building featuring lots of theater and exhibit space, mounts a year-long cycle of inventive puppet productions that change frequently; it also offers puppetry classes.

DINNER THEATER

Copper State Dinner Theatre (6727 N. 47th Ave., Glendale, tel. 623/937–1671), the Valley's oldest troupe, stages light comedy at Max's, a West Valley sports bar, Friday and Saturday nights.

WILD WEST SHOWS

At **Rawhide Western Town & Steakhouse** (23023 N. Scottsdale Rd., Scottsdale, tel. 480/502–1880), the false fronts on the dusty Main Street contain a train depot, saloons, gift shops, and craftspeople. Reenacted Old West shoot-outs and cheesy souvenirs make this a venue for down-home tacky fun. City slickers can take a ride on a stagecoach or gentle burro, and kids will enjoy the Petting Ranch's barnyard animals. Hayrides travel a short distance into the desert for weekend "Sundown Cookouts" under the stars.

Not a Night Owl?

You can learn a lot about a place if you take its pulse after dark. So even if you're the original early-to-bed type, there's every reason to vary your routine when you're away from home.

EXPERIENCE THE FAMILIAR IN A NEW PLACE Whether your thing is going to the movies or going to concerts, it's always different away from home. In clubs, new faces and new sounds add up to a different scene. Or you may catch movies you'd never see at home.

TRY SOMETHING NEW Do something you've never done before. It's another way to dip into the local scene. A simple suggestion: Go out later than usual—go dancing late and finish up with breakfast at dawn.

DO SOMETHING OFFBEAT Look into lectures and readings as well as author appearances in book stores. You may even meet your favorite novelist.

EXPLORE A DAYTIME NEIGHBORHOOD AT NIGHT Take a nighttime walk through an explorable area you've already seen by day. You'll get a whole different view of it.

ASK AROUND If you strike up a conversation with like-minded people during the course of your day, ask them about their favorite spots. Your hotel concierge is another resource.

DON'T WING IT As soon as you've nailed down your travel dates, look into local publications or surf the Net to see what's on the calendar while you're in town. Look for hot regional acts, dance and theater, big-name performing artists, expositions, and sporting events. Then call or click to order tickets.

CHECK OUT THE NEIGHBORHOOD Whenever you don't know the neighborhood you'll be visiting, review safety issues with people in your hotel. What's the transportation situation? Can you walk there, or do you need a cab? Is there anything else you need to know?

CASH OR CREDIT? Know before you go. It's always fun to be surprised—but not when you can't cover your check.

Rockin' R Ranch (6136 E. Baseline Rd., Mesa, tel. 480/832–1539) includes a petting zoo, a reenactment of a wild shoot-out, and—the main attraction—a nightly cookout with a Western stage show. Pan for gold or take a wagon ride until the "vittles" are served, followed by music and entertainment. Similar to its competitor, Rawhide, Rockin' R is a better deal as it's all-inclusive.

In This Chapter

Updated by Cara LaBrie

where to stay

IF THERE'S ONE THING THE VALLEY OF THE SUN KNOWS how to do right, it's lodging. And metropolitan Phoenix has options ranging from world-class resorts to roadside motels, from upscale dude ranches to no-frills family-style operations where you can do your own cooking.

Most resorts lie far from downtown Phoenix, although the renaissance of this area has brought new interest from hoteliers, with historic spots such as the Arizona Biltmore (still Phoenix's nicest) and the charming San Marcos being joined by many others. Most of the other resorts are in the neighboring, tourist-friendly city of Scottsdale, a destination in its own right; a few are scattered 20 to 30 mi to the north in the quickly expanding communities of Carefree and Cave Creek. Dude-ranch territory is 60 mi northwest, in the town of Wickenburg.

Most downtown Phoenix properties are business and family hotels, closer to the heart of the city—and to the average vacationer's budget. Many properties cater to corporate travelers during the week, but lower their rates on weekends to entice leisure travelers; ask about weekend specials when making reservations.

Travelers flee snow and ice to bask in the Valley of the Sun. As a result, winter is the high season, peaking in January through March. Summer season—mid-May through the end of September—is giveaway time, when a night at one of the fanciest resorts often goes for a quarter of the winter price.

CATEGORY	COST*
$$$$	over $250
$$$	$175–$250
$$	$100–$175
$	under $100

*All prices are for a standard double room, excluding room tax

NORTH CENTRAL PHOENIX: BILTMORE DISTRICT

$$$$ ★ **ARIZONA BILTMORE.** Designed by Frank Lloyd Wright's colleague Albert Chase McArthur, the Biltmore has remained the premier resort in central Phoenix since it opened in 1929. The dramatic lobby, with its stained-glass skylights, wrought-iron pilasters, and cozy sitting alcoves, fills with piano music in the evenings, inviting guests to linger. Impeccably manicured grounds have open walkways, fountains, and flower beds in colorful bloom. Story has it that the Catalina Pool's blue and gold tiles so enchanted former owner William Wrigley Jr. that he bought the factory that produced them. Rooms have marble bathrooms and the same low-key elegance as the rest of the hotel, decorated in earth tones and accented with Southwestern-patterned accessories. You'll be in good company: every American president since Herbert Hoover, and various celebrities, have stayed here. *24th St. and Missouri Ave., Phoenix 85016, tel. 602/955–6600 or 800/950–0086, fax 602/381–7600. 720 rooms, 50 villas. 4 restaurants, lobby lounge, 7 pools, 2 18-hole golf courses, putting green, 8 tennis courts, health club, jogging, concierge, car rental, free parking. AE, D, DC, MC, V. www.arizonabiltmore.com*

$$$$ **RITZ-CARLTON.** This sand-color neo-Federal facade facing Biltmore Fashion Park hides a graceful, well-appointed luxury hotel. Large public rooms are decorated with 18th- and 19th-century European paintings and house a handsome china collection. Rooms, done in shades of ice blue and peach, have stocked refrigerators, irons with ironing boards, feather and foam pillows,

safes, and white-marble bath basins. Choose between mountain or city vistas. *2401 E. Camelback Rd., Phoenix 85016, tel. 602/468–0700 or 800/241–3333, fax 602/468–0793. 281 rooms, 14 suites. Restaurant, 3 bars, pool, 2 saunas, exercise room, bicycles, concierge floor, business services, parking (fee). AE, D, DC, MC, V. www.ritzcarlton.com*

$$$ EMBASSY SUITES BILTMORE. Adjacent to Biltmore Fashion Park, this large all-suites hotel has a cheery, informal feel. Huge palms, boulders, and waterfalls punctuate an airy lobby, and mazelike paths lead to lodgings around the atrium. The pleasant suites have small living rooms, larger bedrooms, wet bars, and nicely appointed baths. Complimentary breakfast and afternoon cocktails are thoughtful perks. *2630 E. Camelback Rd., Phoenix 85016, tel. 602/955–3992 or 800/362–2779, fax 602/955–3992. 232 suites. Restaurant, lounge, pool, hot tub, exercise room. AE, D, DC, MC, V. www.embassy-suites.com*

$$–$$$ CAMELBACK COURTYARD BY MARRIOTT. Built in 1990, this four-story hostelry delivers compact elegance in its public areas (lots of plants, white tile, and wood) and reliable, no-frills comfort in its rooms and suites. A lap pool and Jacuzzi await in the landscaped courtyard. More than 50 restaurants are within walking distance. *2101 E. Camelback Rd., Phoenix 85016, tel. 602/955–5200 or 800/321–2211, fax 602/955–1101. 154 rooms, 11 suites. Breakfast room, bar, room service, pool, hot tub, exercise room, meeting rooms, free parking. AE, D, DC, MC, V. www.marriott.com*

$$–$$$ PHOENIX INN. A block off a popular stretch of Camelback Road, this three-story property is a remarkable bargain, considering it has amenities not generally seen in properties of the same price category—leather love seats, refrigerators, coffeemakers, hair dryers, and microwaves. Several rooms have corner Jacuzzis. Continental breakfast is served daily from 6 to 10, in a pleasant breakfast room with a large television. *2310 E. Highland Ave., Phoenix 85016, tel. 602/956–5221 or 800/956–5221, fax 602/468–7220. 120 suites. Breakfast room, pool, hot tub, exercise room, shop, coin laundry. AE, D, DC, MC, V. www.phoenixinn.com*

NORTHEAST PHOENIX AND PARADISE VALLEY

$$$$ **HERMOSA INN.** The ranch-style lodge at the heart of this small
★ resort was the home and studio of cowboy artist Lon Megargee
in the 1930s; today the adobe structure houses **Lon's** (☞ Eating
Out), justly popular for its New American cuisine and amiable staff.
The inn, on 6 acres of lush lawn mixed with desert landscaping,
is a hidden jewel of hospitality and low-key luxury. Villas as big
as private homes and individually decorated casitas hold an
enviable collection of art. The secluded Garden Court's hot tub
is set in a beautifully designed courtyard. A blessedly peaceful
alternative to some of the larger resorts, the Hermosa offers
serenity, attention to detail, and alluring accommodations. 5532
N. Palo Cristi Rd., Paradise Valley 85253, tel. 602/955–8614 or 800/
241–1210, fax 602/955–8299. 4 villas, 3 haciendas, 22 casitas, 17
ranchos. Restaurant, bar, kitchenettes, pool, 2 hot tubs, 3 tennis courts,
free parking. AE, D, DC, MC, V. BP. www.hermosainn.com

$$$$ **ROYAL PALMS.** Once the home of Cunard Steamship executive
Delos T. Cooke, this Mediterranean-style resort has beautifully
maintained courtyards with antique fountains, a stately row of the
namesake palms at its entrance, and individually designed stylish
rooms. The deluxe casitas are each done in a different theme—
Trompe l'Oeil, Romantic Retreat, Spanish Colonial—by members
of the American Society of Interior Designers. The restaurant, **T.
Cook's** (☞ Eating Out), is one of the most popular in town. 5200
E. Camelback Rd., Phoenix 85018, tel. 602/840–3610 or 800/672–
6011, fax 602/840–6927. 116 rooms and casitas, 4 suites. Restaurant,
bar, pool, tennis court, exercise room, business services, meeting rooms,
free parking. AE, D, DC, MC, V. www.royalpalmshotel.com

$$$–$$$$ **DOUBLETREE LA POSADA RESORT.** Camelback Mountain is a
spectacular backdrop for this sprawling resort with extensive
athletic and sports facilities. The vast Lagoon Pool is the resort's
centerpiece, replete with cascading waterfalls, passageways
under red boulder formations, and the Grotto Bar. Large rooms

sport iron furniture and Navajo-patterned bedspreads; all have patios, data ports, and bathrooms with double vanities. The property's tile floors, mauve/maroon carpets, and amusing chandeliers might make you think you're in a time warp (the place was built in 1978), and the lounge's round, sunken disco floor may fulfill your burning, unresolved "Saturday Night Fever" fantasies. *4949 E. Lincoln Dr., Paradise Valley 85253, tel. 602/952–0420 or 800/222–8733, fax 602/840–8576. 252 rooms, 10 suites. Restaurant, lounge, in-room data ports, 2 pools, 4 hot tubs, beauty salon, massage, sauna, 2 putting greens, 6 tennis courts, exercise room, horseshoes, racquetball, volleyball, pro shop, nightclub, free parking. AE, D, DC, MC, V. www.doubletreehotels.com*

CENTRAL PHOENIX

$$–$$$ EMBASSY SUITES PHOENIX AIRPORT WEST. Just minutes from downtown, this four-story courtyard hotel has lush palms and olive trees surrounding bubbling fountains and a sunken pool. Complimentary breakfast, cooked to order, and an evening social hour are offered in the spacious atrium lounge. Rooms have hair dryers, irons and ironing boards, and wet bars with microwaves, sinks, and mini-refrigerators. *2333 E. Thomas Rd., 85016, tel. 602/957–1910, fax 602/955–2861. 183 suites. Restaurant, kitchenettes, refrigerators, pool, hot tub, exercise room, laundry service, airport shuttle, free parking. AE, D, DC, MC, V. BP. www.embassy-suites.com*

$$–$$$ HYATT REGENCY PHOENIX. A quintessential Hyatt, this convention-oriented hotel has a seven-story atrium with huge sculptures, colorful tapestries, potted plants, and comfortable seating areas. Rooms are spacious and comfortable, and there's a revolving restaurant with panoramic views of the Phoenix area. The hotel efficiently handles the arrival and departure of hundreds of business travelers each day. Note: The atrium roof blocks east views on floors 8 to 10. *122 N. 2nd St., 85004, tel. 602/252–1234 or 800/233–1234, fax 602/254–9472. 667 rooms. 45 suites. 4 restaurants,*

2 bars, pool, exercise rooms, concierge, business services, meeting rooms, car rental, parking (fee). AE, D, DC, MC, V. www.hyatt.com

$–$$$ HOTEL SAN CARLOS. Built in 1928, this seven-story hotel is a step back in time: big-band music, wall tapestries, Austrian crystal chandeliers, shiny copper elevators—Phoenix's first—and an accommodating staff transport you to a more genteel era. Among other distinctions, the San Carlos was the Southwest's first air-conditioned hotel, and suites bear the names of such movie star guests as Marilyn Monroe and Spencer Tracy. Rooms, rather snug by modern standards, have attractive period furnishings, plus coffeemakers and complimentary movies (and if you think the rooms are small, wait until you see the pool). 202 N. Central Ave., 85004, tel. 602/253–4121 or 800/678–8946, fax 602/253–6668. 133 rooms. 3 restaurants, café, pool, exercise room, meeting rooms, parking (fee). AE, D, DC, MC, V. www.hotelsancarlos.com

$$ HILTON SUITES. This practical and popular hotel with an 11-story atrium is a model of excellent design within tight limits. It sits off Central Avenue, 2 mi north of downtown amid the Central Corridor cluster of office towers. The marble-floor, pillared lobby opens into an atrium containing palm trees, natural boulder fountains, glass elevators, and a lantern-lighted café, where guests enjoy a bite. Each room has an exercise bike and VCR, and a large walk-through bathroom between the living room and bedroom. 10 E. Thomas Rd., 85012, tel. 602/222–1111 or 800/445–8667, fax 602/265–4841. 226 suites. Restaurant, bar, kitchenettes, refrigerators, in-room VCRs, indoor lap pool, sauna, hot tub, exercise room, free parking. AE, D, DC, MC, V. www.hilton.com

$$ LEXINGTON HOTEL. Phoenix's best bet for fitness enthusiasts and sports-lovers, the Lexington houses a 45,000-square-ft health facility, which includes a full-size indoor basketball court, a 40-station machine workout center, and a large outdoor waterfall pool. The ambience is bright, modern, and informal. Rooms range in size from moderate (in the cabana wing, first-floor rooms have poolside patios) to very small (tower wing). This is where visiting teams—and fans—like to stay. *100 W. Clarendon Ave., 85013, tel. 602/279–9811, fax 602/285–2932. 180 rooms. Sports bar, pool, beauty salon, hot tub, massage, sauna, steam room, health club, basketball, racquetball, free parking. AE, D, DC, MC, V.*

$–$$ QUALITY HOTEL & RESORT. With a 1½-acre Getaway Lagoon ringed by exotic palms and bamboo, the Quality is central Phoenix's best bargain oasis. Rooms and public areas are simply furnished, whereas the VIP floor offers cabana suites and a private rooftop pool with views of downtown Phoenix's ever-changing skyline. Be prepared for occasional lapses in service. *3600 N. 2nd Ave., 85013, tel. 602/248–0222 or 800/256–1237, fax 602/265–6331. 257 rooms, 23 suites. Restaurant, bar, 4 pools, hot tub, putting green, basketball, exercise room, shuffleboard, volleyball, playground, laundry, business services, free parking. AE, D, DC, MC, V. www.getawayresort.com*

NORTH AND WEST PHOENIX

$$$$ WIGWAM RESORT. Built in 1918 as a retreat for executives of the Goodyear Company, the Wigwam has the pleasing feel of an upscale lodge. You'll still find a wealth of perks, primary among them two top-notch designer golf courses. Casita-style rooms, situated along paths overflowing with cacti, palms, and huge bougainvillea, are decorated in a tasteful Southwestern style: distressed-wood furniture, iron lamps, pastel walls, and brightly patterned spreads. Local artwork adorns the walls, and all rooms have patios. The business center is in a separate wing so as to not mix business with pleasure, and the immense suites have parlors that can hold up to 300 of your closest friends. It's easy to see how this isolated world of graciousness inspires a fierce loyalty in its guests, some of whom have been returning for more than 50 years. *300 Wigwam Blvd., Litchfield Park 85340, tel. 623/935–3811 or 800/327–0396, fax 623/935–3737. 261 rooms, 70 suites. 3 restaurants, 3 bars, 2 pools, 2 hot tubs, beauty salon, 3 golf courses, 9 tennis courts, basketball, croquet, exercise room, Ping-Pong, shuffleboard, volleyball,* pro shop, children's programs, business services, meeting room, free parking. AE, D, DC, MC, V. www.wigwamresort.com

$$$–$$$$ POINTE HILTON AT SQUAW PEAK. The most family-oriented of the Pointe group, Squaw Peak features a 9-acre recreation area known as the Hole-in-the-Wall River Ranch with swimming pools fed by man-made waterfalls, a 130-ft water slide, and a 1,000-ft "river" that winds past a miniature golf course, tennis courts, outdoor decks, and artificial buttes with stunning mountain vistas. The Coyote Camp keeps kids busy with activities from gold panning to arts and crafts. Accommodations in the pink stucco buildings vary in size from standard two-room suites to the grand three-bedroom Palacio; all have two or more televisions, wet bars, and balconies. Families prefer the bi-level suites. 7677 N. 16th St., Phoenix 85020, tel. 602/997–2626 or 800/ 876–4683, fax 602/997–2391. 431 suites, 130 casitas, one 3-bedroom house. 3 restaurants, 2 lounges, 7 pools, spa, 18-hole golf course, miniature golf, 3 tennis courts, exercise room, hiking, Ping-Pong, mountain bikes, shops, children's programs, meeting rooms. AE, D, DC, MC, V. www.pointehilton.com

$$–$$$$ POINTE HILTON AT TAPATIO CLIFFS. This oasis, snuggled into 400 acres at the base of Phoenix North Mountain Desert Park, has some of the Valley's most spectacular views. The lobby has an open, airy feel, with beamed chalet-type ceilings, so the bright purple carpeting and bold bedspreads in the rooms come as something of a surprise. But the whitewashed wood furniture, tin mirrors, marble counters, and well-chosen art are all nice touches. The resort's centerpiece is "The Falls," an award-winning 3-acre creation: a 40-ft cascade fed by mountain waterfalls ends in 12 travertine pools, surrounded by tiled terraces and flower gardens. 11111 N. 7th St., 85020, tel. 602/866–7500 or 800/876–4683, fax 602/993–0276. 584 suites. 3 restaurants, 3 lounges, 7 pools, spa, 18-hole golf course, 11 tennis courts, exercise room, hiking, horseback riding, jogging, business services, meeting rooms, airport shuttle, parking (fee). AE, D, DC, MC, V. www.pointehilton.com

NEAR SKY HARBOR AIRPORT

$$$–$$$$ **POINTE HILTON ON SOUTH MOUNTAIN.** The Southwest's largest resort, 15 minutes from downtown, sits next to South Mountain Park, a 16,000-acre desert preserve. Rooms and public areas are serviceable, but the facilities are the real draw: the Pointe offers a premier four-story sports center, four restaurants, and various outdoor activities, from golf and tennis to horseback riding and mountain biking. Landscaped walkways and roads link everything on the 750-acre property; carts and drivers are always on call. 7777 S. Pointe Pkwy., Phoenix 85044, tel. 602/438–9000 or 800/876–4683, fax 602/431–6535. 638 suites. 4 restaurants, 6 pools, saunas, 18-hole golf course, 10 tennis courts, health club, hiking, horseback riding, jogging, racquetball, volleyball, mountain bikes, pro shop, coin laundry, meeting rooms, free parking. AE, D, DC, MC, V. www.pointehilton.com

$$ **DOUBLETREE GUEST SUITES.** In the Gateway Center, just 1½ mi north of the airport, this honeycomb of six-story towers is the best of a dozen choices for the traveler who wants to get off the plane and into a comfortable, centrally located property. Rooms have wet bars with microwaves and refrigerators. Vacationers beware: bedroom furnishings cater to corporate guests traveling light— two-drawer credenzas serve as bureaus and dinky wardrobes function as closets. 320 N. 44th St., Phoenix 85008, tel. 602/225–0500 or 800/800–3098, fax 602/225–0957. 242 suites. Restaurant, bar, pool, sauna, exercise room, meeting rooms, free parking. AE, D, DC, MC, V. www.doubletreehotels.com

$$ **HAMPTON INN AIRPORT.** This four-story, interior-corridor hotel 9 mi from downtown is affordable and accommodating. Rooms are moderate size, appointed with handsome armoires and bright-colored leaf or fish prints for drapes and bedspreads. Free Continental breakfast is available in the lobby, where a good-size television is tuned to the local wake-up news show. Take advantage of the hotel shuttle running from 5 AM to midnight. 4234 S. 48th St., Phoenix 85040, tel. 602/438–8688 or 800/426–7866, fax 602/431–8339. 130 rooms, 4 suites. In-room VCRs, pool, hot tub, jogging, meeting

phoenix and scottsdale lodging

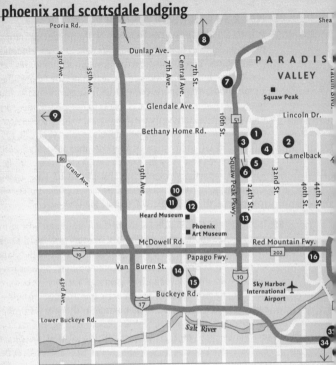

rooms, airport shuttle, free parking. AE, D, DC, MC, V. CP.
www.hamptoninn.com

SCOTTSDALE

$$$$ HYATT REGENCY SCOTTSDALE AT GAINEY RANCH. A fun place
for families, this resort has a huge water park with waterfalls, 10
pools, a water slide, lagoons plied by gondolas, and waterways
that encircle three-quarters of the property. Three golf courses offer
a choice of terrains—dunes, arroyo, or lakes—to suit a fancy for
sand or water traps. The lobby is filled with stunning Native
American sculpture and looks onto a large courtyard where
weekend flamenco guitar performances are held. An innovative
project, the Hopi Center provides exhibits and demonstrations,
presided over by two Hopi Indians—it's a remarkable venture for
a resort, and well worth a visit even for nonguests. Rooms are nicely
sized and comfortable. *7500 E. Doubletree Ranch Rd., 85258, tel. 480/
991–3388 or 800/233–1234, fax 480/483–5550. 493 rooms, 7 casitas.
3 restaurants, 1 bar, 10 pools, 3 9-hole golf courses, 8 tennis courts,
croquet, health club, concierge floor, business services, free parking. AE,
D, DC, MC, V. www.hyatt.com*

$$$$ MARRIOTT'S CAMELBACK INN. This historic resort is a swank oasis
★ of comfort and relaxation in the gorgeous valley between
Camelback and Mummy mountains, with the best-known spa in
the area. Founded in the mid-'30s, the Camelback revels in its
Southwest setting, from the stunning cacti adorning the 125-
acre grounds to the latilla beam/kiva log lodgings. Rooms are
notably spacious and varied in configuration—seven suites even
have private swimming pools. A gallery displays Barry Goldwater's
historic and landscape photographs, a revelation for those who
didn't know of the former senator's talent with a camera. Visit the
acclaimed spa, where you can indulge in a massage or in something
more exotic like a Para-Joba Body Wrap or an Adobe Mud
Purification Treatment. *5402 E. Lincoln Dr., 85253, tel. 480/948–1700
or 800/242–2635, fax 480/951–8469. 453 rooms, 27 suites. 5 restaurants,*

lounge, coffee shop, 3 pools, spa, 2 18-hole golf courses, 6 tennis courts, hiking, business services, meeting rooms, free parking. AE, D, DC, MC, V. www.camelbackinn.com

$$$$ **THE PHOENICIAN.** Guests enter a bright, airy lobby to find
★ towering fountains, gleaming marble, and smiling faces of a service staff who will do handsprings to satisfy. French-provincial decor and authentic Dutch-master paintings are a bit of a surprise in the desert, and create a sumptuous atmosphere. A 2-acre cactus garden showcases hundreds of varieties of cacti and succulents, the Centre for Well Being spa has an inspiring meditation atrium, and the resort's centerpiece pool is lined with mother-of-pearl tiles. Rooms are spacious, with cream walls, tasteful rattan furnishings in muted tones, Italian marble bathrooms, and private patios. Ask for a room facing south, with views of the resort's pools and the city. In a city known for great dining, the Phoenician can lay claim to two of the area's finest restaurants, **Mary Elaine's** and the **Terrace Dining Room** (☞ Eating Out). *6000 E. Camelback Rd., 85251, tel. 480/941–8200 or 800/ 888–8234. 581 rooms, 73 suites. 4 restaurants, 9 pools, barbershop, beauty salon, sauna, steam room, golf privileges, 12 tennis courts, archery, badminton, basketball, croquet, health club, jogging, volleyball, pro shop, billiards, children's programs, business services. AE, D, DC, MC, V. www.thephoenician.com*

$$$$ **SCOTTSDALE PLAZA RESORT.** Arched doorways, soft-beige stucco, and tiered stone fountains lend Old World charm to this hotel's Spanish-Mediterranean ambience. Although it lacks the requisite lush golf fairways, this 40-acre independent hotel is out to compete with the five-star big boys. Special-touch amenities—such as the box of chocolate truffles left on the pillow—accompany more pragmatic luxuries like 2-ft-thick walls between rooms. Suites are arranged around a courtyard pool, and the resort boasts Arizona's largest hot tub. The lounge at **Remington's,** the hotel's main restaurant, features jazz combos. *7200 N. Scottsdale Rd., 85253, tel. 480/948–5000 or 800/832–2025, fax 480/998–5971. 224 rooms, 170* *suites, 10 lodges. 2 restaurants, 3 lounges, 5 pools, beauty salon, 3 outdoor spas, putting green, 5 tennis courts, exercise room, racquetball, pro shop, free parking. AE, D, DC, MC, V. www.scottsdaleplaza.com*

$$$$ SCOTTSDALE PRINCESS. On the 450 beautifully landscaped acres of this resort, Mexican-colonial architecture is set against the splendor of the McDowell Mountains. Built around a series of outdoor areas, the resort has a wonderfully open feel. Rooms in the red-tile-roof main building and the casitas are furnished in desert-sand tones with pink accents; the resort's emphasis on spaciousness is echoed in details like "walk-around" tile showers and immense closets. The **Marquesa** restaurant has been consistently rated one of the best in the state. Another top-notch restaurant is **The Grill at the TPC**, an upscale steak and seafood establishment (☞ Eating Out, for both). The landscape director leads tours of the 450-acre grounds, which are lush with palms, bougainvillea, and rosemary shrubs (each restaurant has its own herb garden). For perfect sunset-gazing, choose the quiet east pool, where the distant mountains are perfectly framed by a circle of palms. *7575 E. Princess Dr., 85255, tel. 480/585–4848 or 800/344–4758, fax 480/585–0091. 650 rooms, 21 suites, 125 casitas, 75 villas. 5 restaurants, bar, 3 pools, spa, steam room, 2 18-hole golf courses, 7 tennis courts, health club, racquetball, squash, pro shops, business services, free parking. AE, D, DC, MC, V. www.fairmont.com*

$$$–$$$$ SUNBURST RESORT. This low-rise hotel may be Scottsdale's best-kept secret. Five two-story structures line grounds dotted with orange trees and Adirondack chairs clustered beneath oversized canvas umbrellas. Roomy accommodations are decorated with patterned bedspreads in vivid, primary colors, benches upholstered in whimsical cow-print material, and intricately carved pine furnishings; French doors open onto private balconies. Motorists will appreciate parking close to the room. *4925 N. Scottsdale Rd., 85251, tel. 480/945–7666 or 800/528–7867, fax 480/945–4056. 205 rooms, 5 suites. Restaurant, bar, pool, refrigerators, exercise room, meeting rooms, free parking. AE, D, DC, MC, V. www.sunburstresort.com*

$$–$$$$ RADISSON RESORT AND SPA. With myriad sports options, this hotel is the perfect match for active types who desire the facilities of a swank resort in a low-key setting. Two-story buildings house guest rooms, accessible via pathways winding through the well-kept grounds. The large, airy lobby has massive fountains. The spacious rooms are done in teal and peach tones, with patios or balconies, big closets, and sitting areas. Tapps, the resort's pub, features 12 specialty beers on draft. *7171 N. Scottsdale Rd., 85253, tel. 480/991–3800 or 800/333–3333, fax 602/948–1381. 318 rooms, 32 bi-level suites, 2 luxury suites. Restaurant, 2 bars, patisserie, 4 pools, beauty salon, spa, 2 18-hole golf courses, 21 tennis courts, volleyball. D, DC, MC, V. www.radisson.com/scottsdaleaz*

$$$ MARRIOTT'S MOUNTAIN SHADOWS. Across the street from the more upscale Camelback Inn, this Marriott property is a ranch-style resort, perfect for families and enviably located, as its name implies, right at the base of Camelback Mountain. Although the furnishings aren't as distinctive as at its high-class sister property, rooms are large and comfortable, with walk-in closets and spacious sitting areas. Creeks and a waterfall make the highly regarded golf course a duffer's oasis; you can even play night golf with glow-in-the-dark balls. If the golf doesn't relax you, head for the two hydrotherapy pools. *5641 E. Lincoln Dr., 85253, tel. 480/948–7111 or 800/228–9290, fax 480/951–5430. 318 rooms, 19 suites. 3 restaurants, lounge, 3 pools, massage, sauna, 18-hole executive golf course, putting green, 8 tennis courts, exercise room, Ping-Pong, pro shop, meeting rooms, airport shuttle, free parking. AE, D, DC, MC, V. www.marriott.com*

$$$ RENAISSANCE COTTONWOODS RESORT. Shopaholics will like this 25-acre resort—it's across the street from the shops and restaurants of the Borgata Shopping Center (☞ Shopping). Check in among pottery and large cacti in the low-key lobby; you'll be chauffeured in a golf cart to your room in one of the adobe buildings. White stucco rooms are pleasant, with light wood furniture, beamed ceilings, and small but well-kept bathrooms. The suites are much grander, boasting private hot tubs, large living rooms, and minibars. 6160 N. Scottsdale Rd., 85253, tel. 480/991–1414, fax 480/951–3350. 64 rooms, 106 villas. Restaurant, 2 pools, 4 tennis courts, meeting rooms. AE, D, DC, MC, V. www.renaissancehotels.com

$ ECONOLODGE SCOTTSDALE. The most attractive feature of this three-story, exterior corridor motel is its location within walking distance of Scottsdale's Old Town and boutique/gallery enclave. Modest rooms have standard but serviceable furnishings that include a sofa, coffee table, and petite writing desk, as well as a large open-closet dressing area. Don't come expecting luxury; what you will find is a friendly welcome and a blessedly short stroll to some of the area's finest shopping—which in this city based on the almighty auto is a rarity. 6935 E. 5th Ave., 85251, tel. 480/994–9461 or 800/528–7396, fax 480/947–1695. 92 rooms. Breakfast room, pool, hot tub, free parking. AE, D, DC, MC, V. www.choicehotels.com

$ MOTEL 6 SCOTTSDALE. The best bargain in Scottsdale lodging is easy to miss, but it's worth hunting for as it's close to the specialty shops of 5th Avenue and Scottsdale's Civic Plaza. Amenities aren't a priority here, but the price is remarkable considering the stylish and much more expensive resorts found close by. Rooms are small and spare with blue carpets, print bedspreads, and a small desk and wardrobe. And how many Motel 6 properties have a pool surrounded by palms and rooms with a view of Camelback Mountain? 6848 E. Camelback Rd., 85251, tel. 480/946–2280 or 800/466–8356, fax 480/949–7583. 122 rooms. Pool, hot tub, free parking. AE, D, DC, MC, V. www.motel6.com

NORTH OF SCOTTSDALE: CAREFREE AND CAVE CREEK

$$$$ THE BOULDERS. The Valley's most serene and secluded luxury ★ resort hides among hill-size, 12-million-year-old granite boulders in the foothills town of Carefree, just over the border from Scottsdale. Casitas snuggled into the rocks have exposed log-beam ceilings, ceiling fans, and curved, pueblo-style half-walls and shelves. Each has a patio with a view, a miniature kiva fireplace, and spacious bathrooms with deep tubs. Luxury touches abound, from champagne on arrival to "couples massages" available in the privacy of your casita. Boutiques and a satellite branch of the Heard Museum are on the property, and golfers stay here to play on two premier courses. *34631 N. Tom Darlington Dr., Carefree 85377, tel. 480/488–9009 or 800/553–1717, fax 480/488–4118. 160 casitas, 46 patio homes. 5 restaurants, 2 pools, spa, 2 18-hole golf courses, 6 tennis courts, exercise room, hiking, horseback riding, jogging, business services, meeting rooms, free parking. AE, D, DC, MC, V. www.grandbay.com*

EAST VALLEY: TEMPE AND MESA

$$$–$$$$ **THE BUTTES.** Two miles east of Sky Harbor, nestled in desert buttes at I–10 and AZ 60, this hotel joins dramatic architecture (the lobby's back wall is the volcanic rock itself) and classic Southwest design (pine and saguaro-rib furniture, works by major regional artists) with stunning Valley views. "Radial" rooms are largest, with the widest views; inside rooms face the huge free-form pools, with waterfall, hot tubs, and poolside cantina. The elegant **Top of the Rock** restaurant (☞ Eating Out) is a definite plus. *2000 Westcourt Way, Tempe 85282, tel. 602/225–9000 or 800/843–1986, fax 602/438–8622. 353 rooms. 2 restaurants, 3 bars, 2 pools, 4 hot tubs, sauna, 4 tennis courts, exercise room, hiking, jogging, bicycles, shop, concierge floor, business services, meeting rooms, free parking. AE, D, DC, MC, V. www.wyndham.com*

$$$ **TEMPE MISSION PALMS HOTEL.** Set between the Arizona State University campus and Old Town Tempe, this three-story courtyard hotel is handy to the East Valley and downtown Phoenix. The tone is set by a handsome, casual lobby—Matisse-inspired upholstery on overstuffed chairs—and an energetic young staff. It's a particularly convenient place to stay if you're attending ASU sports and pro-football Cardinals events (the stadium is virtually next door). Rooms are bright, simple Southwestern, and comfortable. The hotel's "Harry's Bar" becomes a lively sports lounge at game time. *60 E. 5th St., Tempe 85281, tel. 480/894–1400*

Hotel How-Tos

Where you stay does make a difference. Do you prefer a modern high-rise or an intimate B&B? A center-city location or the quiet suburbs? What facilities do you want? Sort through your priorities, then price it all out.

HOW TO GET A DEAL After you've chosen a likely candidate or two, phone them directly and price a room for your travel dates. Then call the hotel's toll-free number and ask the same questions. Also try consolidators and hotel-room discounters. You won't hear the same rates twice. On the spot, make a reservation as soon as you are quoted a price you want to pay.

PROMISES, PROMISES If you have special requests, make them when you reserve. Get written confirmation of any promises.

SETTLE IN Upon arriving, make sure everything works—lights and lamps, TV and radio, sink, tub, shower, and anything else that matters. Report any problems immediately. And don't wait until you need extra pillows or blankets or an ironing board to call housekeeping. Also check out the fire emergency instructions. Know where to find the fire exits, and make sure your companions do, too.

IF YOU NEED TO COMPLAIN Be polite but firm. Explain the problem to the person in charge. Suggest a course of action. If you aren't satisfied, repeat your requests to the manager. Document everything: Take pictures and keep a written record of who you've spoken with, when, and what was said. Contact your travel agent, if he made the reservations.

KNOW THE SCORE When you go out, take your hotel's business cards (one for everyone in your party). If you have extras, you can give them out to new acquaintances who want to call you.

TIP UP FRONT For special services, a tip or partial tip in advance can work wonders.

USE ALL THE HOTEL RESOURCES A concierge can make difficult things easy. But a desk clerk, bellhop, or other hotel employee who's friendly, smart, and ambitious can often steer you straight as well. A gratuity is in order if the advice is helpful.

or 800/547–8705, fax 480/968–7677. 303 rooms. Restaurant, bar, pool, sauna, 3 tennis courts, exercise room, business services, meeting rooms, airport shuttle, free parking. AE, D, DC, MC, V. www.tempemissionpalms.com

$$–$$$ **HILTON PAVILION.** This sand-and-rose-color eight-story property has a Southwestern look. Rooms are medium size, with plum and teal carpeting, average-size baths, small closets, and a large lighted table; corner suites and the top two floors have the best views. The hotel is in the heart of the East Valley, just off AZ 60, and the immense Fiesta Mall is across the street; downtown Phoenix is 18 mi away. *1011 W. Holmes Ave., Mesa 85210, tel. 480/833–5555 or 800/544–5866, fax 480/649–1380. 201 rooms, 62 suites. Restaurant, 2 bars, refrigerators, pool, hot tub, exercise room, business services, free parking. AE, D, DC, MC, V. www.hilton.com*

$$ **TWIN PALMS HOTEL.** Across the street from ASU's Gammage Auditorium and minutes from Old Town Tempe, this seven-story high-rise hotel has a domed-window facade. Faux finishes creatively mask dated, textured walls in the rooms, and corner basins strike strategic blows to cramped bathrooms. Guests receive free admission to facilities at the nearby ASU Recreation Complex with three Olympic-size pools, badminton and squash courts, and aerobics classes. *225 E. Apache Blvd., Tempe 85281, tel. 480/967–9431 or 800/367–0835, fax 480/303–6602. 140 rooms, 1 suite. Bar, pool, concierge floor, airport shuttle, free parking. AE, D, DC, MC, V. www.inovate.com/hpmc/twinpalms*

PRACTICAL INFORMATION

Air Travel

BOOKING

When you book **look for nonstop flights** and **remember that "direct" flights stop at least once.** Try to avoid connecting flights, which require a change of plane.

Several large and small U.S. airlines fly directly to Phoenix. Within Arizona, America West Express/Mesa operates regularly scheduled flights from Phoenix to Flagstaff, Prescott, Lake Havasu, Laughlin, Kingman, Sierra Vista, and Yuma. From the United Kingdom, American Airlines flies from Heathrow via Chicago or from Gatwick via Dallas. Continental Airlines has service from Gatwick via Houston and from Manchester via Newark. Delta flies from London's Gatwick Airport to Phoenix via Atlanta or Cincinnati.

CARRIERS

➤ MAJOR AIRLINES: **Alaska Airlines** (tel. 800/426–0333). **America West** (tel. 800/235–9292). **American** (tel. 800/433–7300). **Continental** (tel. 800/525–0280). **Delta** (tel. 800/221–1212). **Northwest** (tel. 800/225–2525). **TWA** (tel. 800/221–2000). **United** (tel. 800/241–6522). **US Airways** (tel. 800/428–4322).

➤ SMALLER AIRLINES: **America Trans Air** (tel. 800/225–2995). **Frontier Airlines** (tel. 800/432–1359). **Midwest Express** (tel. 800/452–2022). **Southwest** (tel. 800/435–9792).

➤ FROM THE U.K.: **American Airlines** (tel. 0345/789–789). **Continental Airlines** (tel. 0800/776–464 or 01293/776–464). **Delta** (tel. 0800/414–767).

➤ WITHIN ARIZONA: **America West Express/Mesa** (tel. 800/235–9292).

CHECK-IN & BOARDING

Assuming that not everyone with a ticket will show up, airlines routinely overbook planes. When everyone does, airlines ask for volunteers to give up their seats. In return, these volunteers usually get a certificate for a free flight and are rebooked on the next flight out. If there are not enough volunteers, the airline must choose who will be denied boarding. The first to get bumped are passengers who checked in late and those flying on discounted tickets, so **get to the gate and check in as early as possible,** especially during peak periods.

Always **bring a government-issued photo I.D. to the airport.** You may be asked to show it before you are allowed to check in.

CUTTING COSTS

The least expensive airfares to Arizona must usually be purchased in advance and are non-refundable. It's smart to **call a number of airlines, and when you are quoted a good price, book it on the spot**—the same fare may not be available the next day. Always **check different routings** and look into using different airports. Travel agents, especially low-fare specialists, are helpful.

Consolidators are another good source. They buy tickets for scheduled international flights at reduced rates from the airlines, then sell them at prices that beat the best fare available directly from the airlines, usually without restrictions. Sometimes you can even get your money back if you need to return the ticket. Carefully read the fine print detailing penalties for changes and cancellations, and **confirm your consolidator reservation with the airline.**

➤ Consolidators: **Cheap Tickets** (tel. 800/377–1000). **Discount Airline Ticket Service** (tel. 800/576–1600). **Unitravel** (tel. 800/325–2222). **Up & Away Travel** (tel. 212/889–2345). **World Travel Network** (tel. 800/409–6753).

ENJOYING THE FLIGHT

For more legroom, **request an emergency-aisle seat.** Don't sit in the row in front of the emergency aisle or in front of a bulkhead, where seats may not recline. If you have dietary concerns, **ask for special meals when booking.** These can be vegetarian, low-cholesterol, or kosher, for example. On long flights, try to maintain a normal routine, to help fight jet lag. At night, **get some sleep.** By day, **eat light meals, drink water** (not alcohol), and **move around the cabin** to stretch your legs.

FLYING TIMES

Flying time is 5¼ hours from New York, 3½ hours from Chicago, and 1¼ hours from Los Angeles.

HOW TO COMPLAIN

If your baggage goes astray or your flight goes awry, complain right away. Most carriers require that you **file a claim immediately.**

➤ AIRLINE COMPLAINTS: U.S. DEPARTMENT OF TRANSPORTATION Aviation Consumer Protection Division (C-75, Room 4107, Washington, DC 20590, tel. 202/366–2220, www.dot.gov/airconsumer). **Federal Aviation Administration Consumer Hotline** (tel. 800/322–7873).

Airports and Transfers

The area's main gateway is **Phoenix Sky Harbor International,** about 3 mi east of Phoenix city center.

➤ AIRPORT INFORMATION: **Phoenix Sky Harbor International** (24th and Buckeye Sts., off I–10, tel. 602/273–3300).

TRANSFERS BY CAR

It's a 25-minute drive from Sky Harbor to downtown Phoenix and 35-minutes to Glendale or Mesa. Scottsdale can be reached in 30 minutes via AZ 202 east to AZ 101 north.

TRANSFERS BY BUS AND SHUTTLE

Valley Metro buses will get you directly from Terminal 2, 3, or 4 to the bus teminal downtown (at 1st and Washington streets) or to Tempe (Mill and University avenues) in about 20 minutes. For $1.25, with free transfers, the bus can take you from the airport to most other Valley cities (Glendale, Suncity, Scottsdale, etc.) but the trip is likely to be slow.

The blue vans of Supershuttle cruise Sky Harbor, each taking up to seven passengers to their individual destinations, with no luggage fee or airport surcharge. Wheelchair vans are available. Drivers accept credit cards and expect tips.

➤ Bus Information: **Supershuttle** (tel. 602/244–9000 or 800/528–3826). **Valley Metro buses** (tel. 602/253–5000).

TRANSFERS BY LIMOUSINE AND TAXI

Scottsdale Limousine requires reservations but has a toll-free number. Not all taxi firms are licensed to pick up at Sky Harbor's commercail terminals. The licensed companies listed below charge between $8 and $12 for a trip to downtown Phoenix and about $20 to downtown Scottsdale, do not charge for luggage, and are available 24 hours a day.

➤ Limousine and Taxi Information: **Checker/Yellow Cab** (tel. 602/252–5252). **Courier Cab** (tel. 602/232–2222). **Scottsdale Limousine** (tel. 800/747–8234).

Bike Travel

BIKES IN FLIGHT

Most airlines accommodate bikes as luggage, provided they are dismantled and boxed. For bike boxes, often free at bike shops, you'll pay about $5 from airlines (at least $100 for bike bags). International travelers can sometimes substitute a bike for a piece of checked luggage at no charge; otherwise, the cost is about $100. Domestic and Canadian airlines charge $25–$50.

Bus Travel

Valley Metro has 21 express lines and 51 regular routes that reach most of the Valley suburbs. There are no 24-hour routes;

only minimal service is available evenings and Saturdays, and there is no Sunday service. Fares are $1.25 for regular service, $1.75 for express, with free transfers.

The City of Phoenix also runs a 35¢ Downtown Area Shuttle (DASH), with purple minibuses circling the area between the Arizona Center and the state capitol at 15-minute intervals. The City of Tempe operates the Free Local Area Shuttle (FLASH), which serves the downtown Tempe and Arizona State University area from 7 AM until 8 PM. In addition, Dial-a-Ride services, normally reserved for seniors and people with disabilities during the weekdays and on Saturdays, are available on Sundays. Charges begin at $1.20 for the first "zone," or section, of Phoenix in which you travel; each additional zone is 60¢. Greyhound Lines provides service to Phoenix destinations from most parts of the United States.

➤ BUS INFORMATION: **Valley Metro** (tel. 602/253–5000). **Dial-a-Ride** (tel. 602/253–4000). **Greyhound Lines** (tel. 800/231–2222).

Car Rental

Rates in Phoenix begin at $34 a day and $140 a week for an economy car with air-conditioning, an automatic transmission, and unlimited mileage. This does not include tax on car rentals, which is 9.5%.

➤ MAJOR AGENCIES: **Alamo** (tel. 800/522–9696; 020/8759–6200 in the U.K.). **Avis** (tel. 800/331–1084; 800/331–1084in Canada; 02/9353–9000 in Australia; 09/525–1982 in New Zealand). **Budget** (tel. 800/527–0700; 0870/607–5000 in the U.K. through affiliate Europcar). **Dollar** (tel. 800/800–6000; 0124/622–0111 in the U.K., through affiliate Sixt Kenning; 02/9223–1444 in Australia). **Hertz** (tel. 800/654–3001; 800/263–0600 in Canada; 020/8897–2072 in the U.K.; 02/9669–2444 in Australia; 09/256–8690 in New Zealand). **National Car Rental** (tel. 800/227–7368; 020/8680–4800 in the U.K., where it is known as National Europe).

INSURANCE

When driving a rented car you are generally responsible for any damage to or loss of the vehicle as well as for any property damage or personal injury that you may cause. Before you rent see what coverage your personal auto-insurance policy and credit cards already provide.

For about $15 to $20 per day, rental companies sell protection, known as a collision- or loss-damage waiver (CDW or LDW), that eliminates your liability for damage to the car. In Arizona the car-rental company must pay for damage to third parties up to a preset legal limit, beyond which your own liability insurance kicks in. However, **make sure you have enough coverage to pay for the car.** If you do not have auto insurance or an umbrella policy that covers damage to third parties, purchasing liability insurance and a CDW or LDW is highly recommended.

REQUIREMENTS & RESTRICTIONS

In Arizona you must be 21 to rent a car, and rates may be higher if you're under 25. You'll pay extra for child seats (about $3 per day), which are compulsory for children under five, and for additional drivers (about $2 per day). Non-U.S. residents will need a reservation voucher, a passport, a driver's license, and a travel policy that covers each driver, when picking up a car.

Car Travel

Most highways in the state are good to excellent, with easy access, roadside facilities, rest stops, and scenic views. The speed limit on the freeways is now 75 mph, but **don't drive faster than the limit**—police use sophisticated detection systems to catch violators. Distances between destinations may be longer than you are accustomed to, so allow extra time behind the wheel.

At some point you will probably pass through one or more of the state's 23 Native American reservations. Roads and other areas within reservation boundaries are under the jurisdiction of reservation police and governed by separate rules and regulations. **Observe all signs and respect Native Americans' privacy.** Be careful not to hit any animals, which often wander onto the roads; the penalties can be very high.

You must **drive around Phoenix.** Although downtown is pedestrian-friendly, it's difficult to get anywhere else. Mass transit is limited to a bus system which doesn't run on Sundays. Phoenix's approaches from the east and west are I–10, and U.S. 60. Main north–south routes are I–17, I–10, and U.S. 89. Around downtown Phoenix, AZ 202 (Papago Freeway), AZ 143 (Hohokam Freeway), and I–10 (Maricopa Freeway) make an elongated east–west loop, encompassing the state capitol area to the west and Tempe to the east. At mid-loop, AZ 51 (Squaw Peak Parkway) runs north into Paradise Valley. And from the loop's east end, I–10 runs south to Tucson, 100 mi away (although it's still referred to as I–10 east, as it is eventually headed that way); U.S. 60 (Superstition Freeway) branches east to Tempe and Mesa.

Roads in Phoenix and its suburbs are laid out on a single, 800-square-mi grid. Even the freeways run predominantly north–south and east–west. (Grand Avenue, running about 20 mi from northwest downtown to Sun City, is the *only* diagonal.) Central Avenue is the main north–south grid axis: all roads parallel to and west of Central are numbered *avenues*; all roads parallel to and east of Central are numbered *streets*. The numbering begins at Central and increases in each direction.

Weekdays, 6 AM–9 AM and 4 PM–6 PM, the center or left-turn lanes on the major surface arteries of 7th Street and 7th Avenue become one-way traffic-flow lanes between McDowell Road and Dunlap Avenue. These specially marked lanes are dedicated mornings to north–south traffic (into downtown) and afternoons to south–north traffic (out of downtown).

AUTO CLUBS

➤ **IN AUSTRALIA: Australian Automobile Association** (tel. 02/6247–7311).

➤ IN CANADA: **Canadian Automobile Association** (CAA, tel. 613/247–0117).

➤ IN NEW ZEALAND: **New Zealand Automobile Association** (tel. 09/377–4660).

➤ IN THE U.K.: **Automobile Association** (AA, tel. 0990/500–600). **Royal Automobile Club** (RAC, tel. 0990/722–722 for membership; 0345/121–345 for insurance).

➤ IN THE U.S.: **American Automobile Association** (tel. 800/564–6222).

EMERGENCIES
Dial 911 to report accidents on the road and to reach police, the Arizona Department of Public Safety, or fire department.

GASOLINE
Prices vary widely depending on location, oil company, and whether you buy full-serve or self-serve gasoline.

ROAD CONDITIONS
The highways in Arizona are well maintained, however, nature may interfere with your otherwise pleasant drive, bringing mid-July to mid-September dust storms, impromptu flash floods, and immobilizing desert heat. If you're planning to drive through the desert **carry plenty of water, a good spare tire, a jack, and emergency supplies.**

➤ ROAD CONDITIONS: **Arizona Road and Weather Conditions Service** (tel. 602/651–2400 ext. 7623).

RULES OF THE ROAD
Many stretches of freeways permit drivers to travel at 75 mph. In the city, freeway limits are between 55 and 65 mph. Seat belts are required. Tickets can be given for failing to comply. Children under age four must be in child safety seats. Unless otherwise indicated, right turns are allowed on red lights after you've come to a full stop, and left turns onto adjoining one-way streets are

allowed on red lights after you've come to a full stop. Driving with a blood-alcohol level higher than .10 will result in arrest and seizure of driver's license. Fines are severe.

Camera devices are mounted on several street lights to catch speeders and red light runners, and their location is constantly changing. Smart commuters know to avoid Paradise Valley with its low speed limits, and locals swear Indian School is a better street than Camelback for driving between Phoenix and Scottsdale.

Consumer Protection

Whenever shopping or buying travel services in Arizona, **pay with a major credit card** so you can cancel payment or get reimbursed if there's a problem. If you're doing business with a particular company for the first time, **contact your local Better Business Bureau and the attorney general's offices** in your own state and the company's home state, as well. Have any complaints been filed? Finally, if you're buying a package or tour, always **consider travel insurance** that includes default coverage (☞ Insurance, *below*).

▶ **BBBs: Council of Better Business Bureaus** (4200 Wilson Blvd., Suite 800, Arlington, VA 22203, tel. 703/276–0100, fax 703/525–8277 www.bbb.org).

Customs & Duties

When shopping, **keep receipts** for all purchases. Upon reentering the country, **be ready to show customs officials what you've bought.** If you feel a duty is incorrect or object to the way your clearance was handled, note the inspector's badge number and ask to see a supervisor. If the problem isn't resolved, write to the appropriate authorities, beginning with the port director at your point of entry.

IN AUSTRALIA

Australian residents who are 18 or older may bring home $A400 worth of souvenirs and gifts (including jewelry), 250 cigarettes or 250 grams of tobacco, and 1,125 ml of alcohol (including wine, beer, and spirits). Residents under 18 may bring back $A200 worth of goods. Prohibited items include meat products. Seeds, plants, and fruits need to be declared upon arrival.

➤ INFORMATION: **Australian Customs Service** (Regional Director, Box 8, Sydney, NSW 2001, tel. 02/9213–2000, fax 02/9213–4000).

IN CANADA

Canadian residents who have been out of Canada for at least 7 days may bring home C$500 worth of goods duty-free. If you've been away less than 7 days but more than 48 hours, the duty-free allowance drops to C$200; if your trip lasts 24–48 hours, the allowance is C$50. You may not pool allowances with family members. Goods claimed under the C$500 exemption may follow you by mail; those claimed under the lesser exemptions must accompany you. Alcohol and tobacco products may be included in the 7-day and 48-hour exemptions but not in the 24-hour exemption. If you meet the age requirements of the province or territory through which you reenter Canada, you may bring in, duty-free, 1.14 liters (40 imperial ounces) of wine or liquor or 24 12-ounce cans or bottles of beer or ale. If you are 16 or older you may bring in, duty-free, 200 cigarettes and 50 cigars. Check ahead of time with Revenue Canada or the Department of Agriculture for policies regarding meat products, seeds, plants, and fruits.

You may send an unlimited number of gifts worth up to C$60 each duty-free to Canada. Label the package UNSOLICITED GIFT—VALUE UNDER $60. Alcohol and tobacco are excluded.

➤ INFORMATION: **Revenue Canada** (2265 St. Laurent Blvd. S, Ottawa, Ontario K1G 4K3, Canada, tel. 613/993–0534; 800/461–9999 in Canada, fax 613/991–4126, www.ccra-adrc.gc.ca).

IN NEW ZEALAND

Homeward-bound residents 17 or older may bring back $700 worth of souvenirs and gifts. Your duty-free allowance also includes 4.5 liters of wine or beer; one 1,125-ml bottle of spirits; and either 200 cigarettes, 250 grams of tobacco, 50 cigars, or a combination of the three up to 250 grams. Prohibited items include meat products, seeds, plants, and fruits.

➤ INFORMATION: **New Zealand Customs** (Custom House, 50 Anzac Ave., Box 29, Auckland, New Zealand, tel. 09/359–6655, fax 09/359–6732).

IN THE U.K.

From countries outside the EU, including the U.S., you may bring home, duty-free, 200 cigarettes or 50 cigars; 1 liter of spirits or 2 liters of fortified or sparkling wine or liqueurs; 2 liters of still table wine; 60 ml of perfume; 250 ml of toilet water; plus £136 worth of other goods, including gifts and souvenirs. If returning from outside the EU, prohibited items include meat products, seeds, plants, and fruits.

➤ INFORMATION: **HM Customs and Excise** (Dorset House, Stamford St., Bromley, Kent BR1 1XX, tel. 0171/202–4227).

IN THE U.S.

➤ INFORMATION: **U.S. Customs Service** (1300 Pennsylvania Ave. NW, Washington, DC 20229, www.customs.gov; inquiries tel. 202/354–1000; complaints c/o Office of Regulations and Rulings; registration of equipment c/o Resource Management, tel. 202/927–0540).

Dining

The restaurants we list are the cream of the crop in each price category.

RESERVATIONS & DRESS

Reservations are always a good idea: we mention them only when they're essential or not accepted. We mention dress only when men are required to wear a jacket or a jacket and tie.

WINE, BEER & SPIRITS

Possession and consumption of alcoholic beverages is illegal on Indian reservations.

Disabilities & Accessibility

➤ LOCAL RESOURCES: **Southern Arizona Group Office** (tel. 602/640–5250) for information on accessible facilities at specific parks and sites in Arizona.

Gay & Lesbian Travel

Although there are no state-wide gay and lesbian oriented travel organizations in Arizona, the agencies listed below can help plan gay-friendly vacations.

When planning your trip, check out *Fodor's Gay Guide to the USA* (**Fodor's Travel Publications**, tel. 800/533–6478 or in bookstores); $20.

➤ GAY- & LESBIAN-FRIENDLY TRAVEL AGENCIES: **Different Roads Travel** (8383 Wilshire Blvd., Suite 902, Beverly Hills, CA 90211, tel. 323/651–5557 or 800/429–8747, fax 323/651–3678). **Kennedy Travel** (314 Jericho Turnpike, Floral Park, NY 11001, tel. 516/352–4888 or 800/237–7433, fax 516/354–8849, www.kennedytravel.com). **Now Voyager** (4406 18th St., San Francisco, CA 94114, tel. 415/626–1169 or 800/255–6951, fax 415/626–8626, www.nowvoyager.com). **Skylink Travel and Tour** (1006 Mendocino Ave., Santa Rosa, CA 95401, tel. 707/546–9888 or 800/225–5759, fax 707/546–9891, www.skylinktravel.com), serving lesbian travelers.

➤ LOCAL PUBLICATIONS: *Echo* (tel. 602/266–0550) is a gay and lesbian news and entertainment magazine published biweekly and distributed throughout the Southwest and southern California.

Heatstroke (tel. 602/264–3646) is a Phoenix-based biweekly. The weekly **Observer** (tel. 520/622–7176) covers the Tucson and Phoenix area.

Insurance

The most useful travel insurance plan is a comprehensive policy that includes coverage for trip cancellation and interruption, default, trip delay, and medical expenses (with a waiver for preexisting conditions).

Without insurance you will lose all or most of your money if you cancel your trip, regardless of the reason. Default insurance covers you if your tour operator, airline, or cruise line goes out of business. Trip-delay covers expenses that arise because of bad weather or mechanical delays. Study the fine print when comparing policies.

British and Australian citizens need extra medical coverage when traveling overseas.

Always **buy travel policies directly from the insurance company;** if you buy them from a cruise line, airline, or tour operator that goes out of business you probably will not be covered for the agency or operator's default, a major risk. Before making any purchase, **review your existing health and home-owner's policies** to find what they cover away from home.

➤ TRAVEL INSURERS: IN THE U.S.: **Access America** (6600 W. Broad St., Richmond, VA 23230, tel. 804/285–3300 or 800/284–8300, fax 804/673–1583, www.previewtravel.com), **Travel Guard International** (1145 Clark St., Stevens Point, WI 54481, tel. 715/345–0505 or 800/826–1300, fax 800/955–8785, www.noelgroup.com). In Canada: **Voyager Insurance** (44 Peel Center Dr., Brampton, Ontario L6T 4M8, tel. 905/791–8700; 800/668–4342 in Canada).

➤ INSURANCE INFORMATION: IN THE U.K.: **Association of British Insurers** (51–55 Gresham St., London EC2V 7HQ, tel. 0171/600–

3333, fax 0171/696–8999, www.abi.org.uk). In Australia: **Insurance Council of Australia** (tel. 03/9614–1077, fax 03/9614–7924).

Lodging

The lodgings we list are the cream of the crop in each price category. We always list the facilities that are available—but we don't specify whether they cost extra.

Assume that hotels operate on the **European Plan** (EP, with no meals) unless we specify that they use the **Continental Plan** (CP, with a Continental breakfast), **Modified American Plan** (MAP, with breakfast and dinner), or the **Full American Plan** (FAP, with all meals).

APARTMENT & VILLA RENTALS

If you want a home base that's roomy enough for a family and comes with cooking facilities, **consider a furnished rental.**

➤ INTERNATIONAL AGENTS: **Hideaways International** (767 Islington St., Portsmouth, NH 03801, tel. 603/430–4433 or 800/843–4433, fax 603/430–4444, www.hideaways.com; membership $99).

B&BS

➤ RESERVATION SERVICES: **Arizona Association of Bed and Breakfast Inns** (Box 7186, Phoenix 85012, tel. 800/284–2589). **Arizona Trails Bed & Breakfast Reservation Service** (Box 18998, Fountain Hills 85269, tel. 602/837–4284 or 888/799–4282). **Bed & Breakfast Southwest** (P.O. Box 51198, Phoenix 85076, tel. 602/706–8820; 800/762–9704; 602/874–1316 outside AZ). **Mi Casa Su Casa** (Box 950, Tempe 85280, tel. 602/990–0682 or 800/456–0682, fax 602/990–3390; http://www.mi-casa.org). The Arizona Office of Tourism (☞ Visitor Information, *below*) has a statewide list of bed-and-breakfasts.

HOSTELS

No matter what your age, you can **save on lodging costs by staying at hostels.**

➤ **ORGANIZATIONS: Hostelling International—American Youth Hostels** (733 15th St. NW, Suite 840, Washington, DC 20005, tel. 202/783–6161, fax 202/783–6171, www.hiayh.org). **Hostelling International—Canada** (400–205 Catherine St., Ottawa, Ontario K2P 1C3, tel. 613/237–7884, fax 613/237–7868, www.hostellingintl.ca). **Youth Hostel Association of England and Wales** (Trevelyan House, 8 St. Stephen's Hill, St. Albans, Hertfordshire AL1 2DY, tel. 01727/855215 or 01727/845047, fax 01727/844126, www.yha.uk). **Australian Youth Hostel Association** (10 Mallett St., Camperdown, NSW 2050, tel. 02/9565–1699, fax 02/9565–1325, www.yha.com.au). **Youth Hostels Association of New Zealand** (Box 436, Christchurch, New Zealand, tel. 03/379–9970, fax 03/365–4476, www.yha.org.nz).

HOTELS

Most major hotel chains are represented in Arizona. All hotels listed have private bath unless otherwise noted.

➤ **TOLL-FREE NUMBERS: Baymont Inns** (tel. 800/428–3438, www.baymontinns.com). **Best Western** (tel. 800/528–1234, www.bestwestern.com). **Choice** (tel. 800/221–2222, www.hotelchoice.com). **Clarion** (tel. 800/252–7466, www.choicehotels.com). **Colony** (tel. 800/777–1700, www.colony.com). **Comfort** (tel. 800/228–5150, www.comfortinn.com). **Days Inn** (tel. 800/325–2525. www.daysinn.com). **Doubletree and Red Lion Hotels** (tel. 800/222–8733, www.doubletreehotels.com). **Embassy Suites** (tel. 800/362–2779, www.embassysuites.com). **Fairfield Inn** (tel. 800/228–2800, www.marriott.com). **Four Seasons** (tel. 800/332–3442, www.fourseasons.com). **Hilton** (tel. 800/445–8667, www.hiltons.com). **Holiday Inn** (tel. 800/465–4329, www.holiday-inn.com). **Howard Johnson** (tel. 800/654–4656, www.hojo.com). **Hyatt Hotels & Resorts** (tel. 800/233–1234, www.hyatt.com). **La Quinta** (tel. 800/531–5900, www.laquinta.com). **Marriott** (tel. 800/228–9290, www.marriott.com). **Omni** (tel. 800/843–6664, www.omnihotels.com). **Quality Inn** (tel. 800/228–5151, www.qualityinn.com). **Radisson** (tel. 800/

333–3333, www.radisson.com). **Ramada** (tel. 800/228–2828. www.ramada.com), **Renaissance Hotels & Resorts** (tel. 800/468–3571, www.hotels.com). **Sheraton** (tel. 800/325–3535, www.sheraton.com).**Sleep Inn** (tel. 800/753–3746, www.sleepinn.com). **Westin Hotels & Resorts** (tel. 800/228–3000, www.starwood.com). **Wyndham Hotels & Resorts** (tel. 800/822-4200, www.wyndham.com).

MOTELS
➤ TOLL-FREE NUMBERS: **Econo Lodge** (tel. 800/553–2666). **Friendship Inns** (tel. 800/453–4511). **Motel 6** (tel. 800/466–8356). **Rodeway** (tel. 800/228–2000). **Super 8** (tel. 800/848–8888).

Media

NEWSPAPERS & MAGAZINES
Major Arizona-interest publications available state-wide are: *Arizona Business*, *Arizona Highways*, and *Sunset Magazine*. For on-line information, *see* Web Sites, *below*.

Money Matters

Prices throughout this guide are given for adults. Substantially reduced fees are almost always available for children, students, and senior citizens. For information on taxes, *see* Taxes, *below*.

ATMS
Cirrus (tel. 800/424–7787). **Plus** (tel. 800/843–7587) for locations in the U.S. and Canada, or visit your local bank.

CREDIT CARDS
Throughout this guide, the following abbreviations are used: **AE**, American Express; **D**, Discover; **DC**, Diner's Club; **MC**, Master Card; and **V**, Visa.

➤ REPORTING LOST CARDS: **American Express:** tel. 800/528–4800; **Diner's Club:** tel. 800/234–6377; **Discover:** tel. 800/347–2683; **MasterCard:** tel. 800/307–7309; **Visa:** tel. 800/362–7257.

Packing

Wear casual clothing in Arizona. When in more elegant restaurants in larger cities, as well as in dining rooms of some resorts, most men wear jackets, and dressy casual wear is appropriate for women even in the nicest places.

Stay cool in cotton fabrics and light colors. T-shirts, polo shirts, sundresses, and lightweight shorts, trousers, skirts, and blouses are useful year-round in the south. **Bring sun hats, swimsuits, sandals, and sunscreen**—mandatory warm-weather items. **Bring a sweater and a warm jacket in winter,** particularly for high-country travel. And **don't forget jeans and sneakers or sturdy walking shoes**; they're important year-round.

In your carry-on luggage, **pack an extra pair of eyeglasses or contact lenses** and **enough of any medication you take** to last the entire trip. You may also ask your doctor to write a spare prescription using the drug's generic name, since brand names may vary from country to country. In luggage to be checked, **never pack prescription drugs or valuables.** To avoid customs delays, carry medications in their original packaging. And don't forget to carry with you the addresses of offices that handle refunds of lost traveler's checks.

CHECKING LUGGAGE

How many carry-on bags you can bring with you is up to the airline, but most allow two. If you are flying internationally, note that baggage allowances may be determined not by piece but by weight—generally 88 pounds (40 kilograms) in first class, 66 pounds (30 kilograms) in business class, and 44 pounds (20 kilograms) in economy.

Before departure, **itemize your bags' contents** and their worth, and label the bags with your name, address, and phone number. (If you use your home address, cover it so potential thieves can't see it readily.) Inside each bag, **pack a copy of your itinerary.** At check-in, **make sure that each bag is correctly tagged** with the destination airport's three-letter code. If your bags arrive damaged or fail to arrive at all, file a written report with the airline before leaving the airport.

Passports & Visas

➤ **CONTACTS: U.S. Embassy Visa Information Line** (tel. 01891/200–290; calls cost 49p per minute, 39p per minute cheap rate) for U.S. visa information. **U.S. Embassy Visa Branch** (5 Upper Grosvenor Sq., London W1A 1AE) for U.S. visa information; send a self-addressed, stamped envelope. **U.S. Consulate General** (Queen's House, Queen St., Belfast BTI 6EO) if you live in Northern Ireland. **Office of Australia Affairs** (59th floor, MLC Centre, 19–29 Martin Pl., Sydney, NSW 2000) if you live in Australia. **Office of New Zealand Affairs** (29 Fitzherbert Terr., Thorndon, Wellington) if you live in New Zealand.

PASSPORT OFFICES

The best time to apply for a passport or to renew is in fall and winter. Before any trip, check your passport's expiration date, and, if necessary, renew it as soon as possible.

➤ **AUSTRALIAN CITIZENS: Australian Passport Office** (tel. 131–232, www.dfat.gov.au/passports).

➤ **CANADIAN CITIZENS: Passport Office** (tel. 819/994–3500 or 800/567–6868, www.dfait-maeci.gc.ca/passport).

➤ **NEW ZEALAND CITIZENS: New Zealand Passport Office** (tel. 04/494–0700, www.passports.govt.nz).

➤ **U.K. CITIZENS: London Passport Office** (tel. 0990/210–410) for fees and documentation requirements and to request an emergency passport.

➤ **U.S. CITIZENS: National Passport Information Center** (tel. 900/225–5674; calls are 35¢ per minute for automated service, $1.05 per minute for operator service).

Taxes

SALES TAX
Arizona state sales tax, which applies to all purchases except food, is 5%. Phoenix and Tucson levy city sales taxes of 2% and Flagstaff taxes purchases at a rate of 1.8%. Sales taxes do not apply on Indian reservations.

Time

Arizona sets its clocks to mountain standard time—two hours earlier than eastern standard, one hour later than Pacific standard. However, from April to October, when other states switch to daylight saving time, Arizona does not change its clocks; during this portion of the year, the mountain standard hour in Arizona is the same as the Pacific daylight hour in California. To complicate matters, the vast Navajo reservation in the northeastern section of the state *does* observe daylight saving time, so that from April to October it's an hour later on the reservation than it is in the rest of the state. Finally, the Hopi reservation, whose borders fall within those of the Navajo reservation, stays on the same non-Navajo, non–daylight saving clock as the remainder of the state.

Guided Tours

Reservations for tours are a must all year. All tours provide pickup services at area resorts.

ORIENTATION TOURS
Gray Line Tours gives seasonal, three-hour narrated tours including downtown Phoenix, the Arizona Biltmore hotel, Camelback Mountain, mansions in Paradise Valley, Arizona State University, Papago Park, and Scottsdale's Old Town for about $30. Open Road Tours offers excursions to Sedona and the Grand Canyon, Phoenix city tours, and Native American–culture trips to the Salt River Pima–Maricopa Indian Reservation.

For $38, Vaughan's Southwest Custom Tours gives a 4½-hour city tour for 11 or fewer passengers in custom vans, stopping at the Heard Museum, the Arizona Biltmore, and the state capitol building. Vaughan's will also take you east of Phoenix on the Apache Trail. The tour is offered on Tuesday, Friday, and Saturday; the cost is $65.

➤ **INFORMATION: Gray Line Tours** (Box 21126, Phoenix 85036, tel. 602/495–9100 or 800/732–0327). **Open Road Tours** (748 E. Dunlap, No. 2, Phoenix 85020, tel. 602/997–6474 or 800/766–7117). **Vaughan's Southwest Custom Tours** (Box 31250, Phoenix 85046, tel. 602/971–1381 or 800/513–1381).

SPECIAL-INTEREST TOURS

Arizona Carriage Company leads 15-minute to one-hour horse-drawn-carriage tours around Old Scottsdale for $20–$80. Cimarron Adventures and River Co. arranges half-day float trips down the Salt and Verde rivers for about $35 per person. Desert Storm Hummer Tours conducts four-hour nature tours for $90 per person, climbing 4,000 feet up the rugged trails of Tonto National Forest via Hummer.

➤ **INFORMATION: Arizona Carriage Company** (7228 E. 2nd St., Scottsdale 85251, tel. 480/423–1449). **Cimarron Adventures and River Co.** (7901 E. Pierce St., Scottsdale 85257, tel. 480/994–1199). **Desert Storm Hummer Tours** (15525 N. 83rd Way, No. 8, Scottsdale 85260, tel. 480/922–0020).

WALKING TOUR

A 45-minute self-guided walking tour of Old Scottsdale takes you to 14 historic sites in the area. Pick up a map of the route in the Scottsdale Chamber of Commerce (☞ Visitor Information, *below*).

Train Travel

The *Southwest Chief* operates daily between Los Angeles and Chicago, stopping in Kingman, Flagstaff, and Winslow. The

Sunset Limited travels three times each week between Los Angeles and Miami, with stops at Yuma, Tucson, and Benson. There is a connecting Amtrak bus (a two-hour trip) between Tucson and Phoenix. For details, contact Amtrak.

➤ INFORMATION: **Amtrak** (tel. 800/872–7245).

Visitor Information

➤ TOURIST INFORMATION: **Arizona Office of Tourism** (2702 N. Third St., Ste. 4015, Phoenix 85004, tel. 602/230–7733 or 888/520–3434, fax 602/240–5475). **Scottsdale Chamber of Commerce** (7343 Scottsdale Mall, tel. 480/945–8481 or 800/877–1117) is open weekdays 8:30–6:30, Saturday 10–5, and Sunday 11–5.

➤ NATIVE AMERICAN ATTRACTIONS: **Hopi Tribe Office of the Chairman** (Box 123, Kykotsmovi 86039, tel. 520/734–2441, fax 520/734–2435). **Navajo Nation Tourism Office** (Box 663, Window Rock 86515, tel. 520/871–6436, 871–7371, or 871–6659, fax 520/871–7381).

Web Sites

Do check out the World Wide Web when you're planning. You'll find everything from current weather forecasts to virtual tours of famous cities. Fodor's Web site, www.fodors.com, is a great place to start your on-line travels.

➤ GENERAL INFORMATION: The **Arizona Guide** (www.arizonaguide.com) is the official Web site of the Arizona Office of Tourism.

➤ GRAND CANYON: Everything you always wanted to know about this natural wonder can be found at **The Canyon** (www.thecanyon.com), the official Web site of the Grand Canyon Chamber of Commerce.

➤ THE GREAT OUTDOORS: The **Arizona State Parks Web Site** (www.pr.state.az.us) lists basics such as fees and hours for all parks, as well as information about wildlife preservation and listings of special events.

► NEWSPAPER: *Phoenix New Times* (www.phoenixnewtimes.com) maintains a site with lively features and and insiders' guides to dining, the arts, and nightlife in the Phoenix metro area.

When to Go

When you travel to Arizona depends on whether you prefer scorching desert or snowy slopes, elbow-to-elbow resorts, or wide-open territory. Our advice: **Visit during spring and autumn,** when the temperatures are milder and the crowds have thinned out.

Winter is prime time in the central and southern parts of the state. The weather is sunny and mild, and the cities bustle with travelers escaping the cold. Conversely, northern Arizona—including the Grand Canyon—can be wintry, with snow, freezing rain, and subzero temperatures; the road to the Grand Canyon's North Rim is closed during this time.

Arizona's desert regions sizzle in summer, and travelers and their vehicles should be adequately prepared. Practically every restaurant and accommodation is air-conditioned, though, and you can get great deals on tony southern Arizona resorts you might not be able to afford in high season. Summer is also a delightful time to visit northern Arizona's high country, when temperatures are 18°F–20°F lower than they are down south—but hotel prices are commensurately high.

Dehydration, an underestimated danger, can be very serious, especially considering that one of the first major symptoms is the inability to swallow. To avoid this **drink every 10–15 minutes,** up to a gallon of water per day in summer.

Wear a hat and sunglasses and put on sunblock to protect against the burning Arizona sun. And **watch out for heatstroke.** Symptoms include headache, dizziness, and fatigue, which can turn into convulsions and unconsciousness and can lead to death. If someone in your party develops any of these conditions, have one person seek emergency help while others move the victim into the shade, wrap him or her in wet clothing to cool him or her down.

CLIMATE

Phoenix averages 300 sunny days and 7 inches of precipitation annually. Tucson gets all of 11 inches of rain each year, and the high mountains see about 25 inches. The Grand Canyon is usually cool on the rim and about 20°F warmer on the floor. During winter months, approximately 6–12 inches of snow falls on the North Rim; the South Rim receives half that amount.

➤ **Forecasts: Weather Channel Connection** (tel. 900/932–8437), 95¢ per minute from a Touch-Tone phone.

The following average daily maximum and minimum temperatures for two major cities in Arizona offer a representative range of temperatures in the state.

PHOENIX

Jan.	64F	18C	May	89F	32C	Sept.	96F	36C
	37	3		57	14		68	20
Feb.	68F	20C	June	98F	37C	Oct.	84F	29C
	39	4		66	19		57	14
Mar.	73F	23C	July	101F	38C	Nov.	73F	23C
	44	7		73	23		44	7
Apr.	82F	28C	Aug.	96F	36C	Dec.	66F	19C
	51	11		71	22		39	4

FESTIVALS AND SEASONAL EVENTS

➤ **Jan. 1:** Tempe's nationally televised **Fiesta Bowl Footbowl Classic** (tel. 602/350–0911) kicks off the year with a match between the nation's top two college teams.

➤ **Jan.:** At the **Phoenix Open Golf Tournament** (tel. 602/870–4431) in Scottsdale, top players compete at the Tournament Players Club.

➤ **Jan.–Feb.: Parada del Sol Rodeo and Parade** (tel. 602/945–8481), a popular state attraction on Scottsdale Road, features lots of dressed-up cowboys and cowgirls, plus horses and floats.

➤ **MAR.:** In Phoenix, the **Heard Museum Guild Indian Fair and Market** (tel. 602/252–8848) is a prestigious juried show of Native American arts and crafts. Visitors can also enjoy Native American foods, music, and dance.

➤ **MAR.:** The highlight of the **Ostrich Festival** (tel. 602/963–4571) in Chandler is a race of the big birds; it also features a parade, live entertainment, crafts, and food.

➤ **MAR.:** For the **Lost Dutchman Gold Mine Superstition Mountain Trek** (tel. 602/258–6016) in Apache Junction, the Dons of Arizona search for the legendary lost mine, pan for gold, and eat lots of barbecue to keep up their strength. There are crafts demonstrations and fireworks, too.

➤ **Nov.:** During the **Thunderbird Hot-Air-Balloon Classic** (tel. 602/978–7208), 150 or more balloons participate in Scottsdale's colorful race.

➤ **DEC.:** For the three days of **Old Town Tempe Fall Festival of the Arts** (tel. 602/967–4877), the downtown area closes to traffic for art exhibits, food booths, music, and other entertainment.

INDEX

FODOR'S POCKET PHOENIX & SCOTTSDALE

EDITORS: David Downing, Kirsten Weisenberger

EDITORIAL CONTRIBUTOR: Cara LaBrie

Editorial Production: Ira-Neil Dittersdorf

Maps: David Lindroth, *cartographer*; Bob Blake and Rebecca Baer, *map editors*

Design: Fabrizio La Rocca, *creative director*; Tigist Getachew, *art director*; Melanie Marin, *photo editor*

Production/Manufacturing: Angela L. McLean

Cover Photograph: (Teddy Bear Cholla Cactus near Phoenix): Phil Schermeister/Corbis

IMPORTANT TIP

Although all prices, opening times, and other details in this book are based on information supplied to us at press time, changes occur all the time in the travel world, and Fodor's cannot accept responsibility for facts that become outdated or for inadvertent errors or omissions. So **always confirm information when it matters**, especially if you're making a detour to visit a specific place.

SPECIAL SALES

Fodor's Travel Publications are available at special discounts for bulk purchases for sales promotions or premiums. Special editions, including personalized covers, excerpts of existing guides, and corporate imprints, can be created in large quantities for special needs. For more information, contact your local bookseller or write to Special Markets, Fodor's Travel Publications, 280 Park Avenue, New York, NY 10017. Inquiries from Canada should be directed to your local Canadian bookseller or sent to Random House of Canada, Ltd., Marketing Department, 2775 Matheson Boulevard East, Mississauga, Ontario L4W 4P7. Inquiries from the United Kingdom should be sent to Fodor's Travel Publications, 20 Vauxhall Bridge Road, London SW1V 2SA, England.

PRINTED IN THE UNITED STATES OF AMERICA

10 9 8 7 6 5 4 3 2 1